1000 THINGS YOU SHOULD KNOW ABOUT

SPACE

SPACE

John Farndon

Miles Kelly
PUBLISHING

**This edition first published in 2003 for
Books are Fun**

First published in 2000 by
Miles Kelly Publishing,
Bardfield Centre, Great Bardfield, Essex, CM7 4SL, U.K.
Copyright © Miles Kelly Publishing 2000, 2003

2 4 6 8 10 9 7 5 3 1

Library of Congress Cataloging-in-Publication Data
on file at the Library of Congress

ISBN 1-902947-31-2

Editorial Director: Anne Marshall
Editors: Amanda Learmonth, Jenni Rainford
Assistant: Liberty Newton
Americanization: Cindy Leaney
Written and designed by: John Farndon and Angela Koo

Printed in China

CONTENTS

KEY

🌙 Earth, Sun, and Moon

🪐 Planets

✦ Stars

Ⓤ Universe

🔭 Astronomy

🚀 Space travel

Small stars

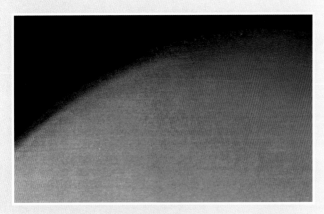

- **Small stars** of low brightness (see H-R diagram) are called white, red, or black dwarves, depending on their color.

- **Red dwarves** are bigger than the planet Jupiter but smaller than our medium-sized star, the Sun. They glow faintly, with 0.01 percent of the Sun's brightness.

- **No red dwarf** can be seen with the naked eye—not even the nearest star to the Sun, the red dwarf Proxima Centauri.

- **White dwarves** are the last stage in the life of a medium-sized star. Although they are even smaller than red dwarves, no bigger than the Earth, they contain the same amount of matter as the Sun.

- **Our night sky's brightest star**, Sirius, the Dog Star,

- ◀ *Black dwarves are stars that were either not big enough to start shining, or which have burned up all their nuclear fuel and stopped glowing, like a coal cinder.*

  has a white dwarf companion called the Pup Star.

- **The white dwarf Omicron-2 Eridani** (also called 40 Eridani) is one of the few dwarf stars that can be seen from the Earth with the naked eye.

- **Brown dwarves** are very cool space objects, little bigger than Jupiter.

- **Brown dwarves** formed in the same way as other stars, but were not big enough to start shining properly. They just glow very faintly with the heat left over from their formation.

- **Black dwarves** are very small, cold, dead stars.

- **The smallest kind of star** is called a neutron star.

Life

- **Life is only known** to exist on Earth, but in 1986 NASA found what they thought might be fossils of microscopic living things in a rock from Mars.

- **Life on Earth** probably began 3.8 billion years ago.

- **The first life forms** were probably bacteria which lived in very hot water around underwater volcanoes.

▲ *Saturn's moon Titan has plenty of evidence of organic (life) chemicals in its atmosphere.*

> **! NEWS FLASH !**
> Microscopic organisms have been found in rock deep underground. Could similar organisms be living under the surface of Mars or Titan?

- **Most scientists** say life's basic chemicals formed on Earth. The astronomer Fred Hoyle said they came from Space.

- **Basic organic (life) chemicals** such as amino acids have been detected in nebulae and meteorites (see Meteors).

- **Huge lightning flashes** may have caused big organic molecules to form on the young Earth.

- **Earth is right for life** because of its gas atmosphere, surface water, and moderately warm temperatures.

- **Mars is the only** other planet that once had water on its surface—which is why scientists are looking for signs of life there.

- **Jupiter's moon Europa** probably has water below its surface which could spawn life.

Space suits

- **Space suits protect astronauts** when they go outside their spacecraft. The suits are also called EMUs (Extra-vehicular Mobility Units).

- **The outer layers** of a space suit protect against harmful radiation from the Sun and bullet-fast particles of space dust called micrometeoroids.

- **The clear, plastic helmet** also protects against radiation and micrometeoroids.

- **Oxygen is circulated** around the helmet to stop the visor misting.

- **The middle layers** of a space suit are blown up to gently hold the astronaut's body. Small astronauts actually have room to "float" inside their space suits.

- **The soft inner lining** of a space suit has tubes of water in it to cool the astronaut's body or warm it up.

- **The backpack** supplies pure oxygen for the astronaut to breathe, and gets rid of the carbon dioxide he or she gives out. The oxygen comes from tanks which hold enough for up to seven hours.

- **The gloves** have silicone-rubber fingertips which allow the astronaut some sense of touch.

- **Various different gadgets** in the suit deal with liquids—including a tube for drinks and another for collecting urine.

- **The full cost** of a spacesuit is about $11 million although 70 percent of this is for the backpack and control module.

◀ Space suits not only have to provide a complete life-support system (oxygen, water, and so on), but must also protect against the dangers of space.

Newton

- **Isaac Newton** (1642–1722) was the scientist who discovered the force of gravity and the laws of motion.

- **Newton's ideas** were inspired by seeing an apple fall from a tree in the garden of his home in England.

- **Newton also discovered** that sunlight can be split into a spectrum made of all the colors of the rainbow.

- **Newton's discovery** of gravity showed why things fall to the ground and planets orbit the Sun.

- **Newton realized** that a planet's orbit depends on its mass and its distance from the Sun.

- **The further apart** and the lighter two objects are, the weaker is the pull of gravity between them.

- **Newton worked out** that you can calculate the pull of gravity between two objects by multiplying their mass by the square of the distance between them.

- **This calculation** allows astronomers to predict precisely the movement of every planet, star, and galaxy in the Universe.

- **Using Newton's formula for gravity**, astronomers have detected previously unknown stars and planets, including Neptune and Pluto, from the effect of their gravity on other space objects.

- **Newton's three laws of motion** showed that every single movement in the Universe can be calculated mechanically.

▶ Newton's theory of gravity showed for the first time why the Moon stays in its orbit around the Earth, and how the gravitational pull between the Earth and the Moon could be worked out mathematically.

Nebulae

◀ This is a glowing nebulae called the Lagoon nebulae, which glows as hydrogen and helium gas in it is heated by radiation from stars.

- **Nebula** (plural nebulae) was the word once used for any fuzzy patch of light in the night sky. Nowadays, many nebulae are known to be galaxies instead.

- **Many nebulae** are huge clouds of gas and space dust.

- **Glowing nebulae** are named because they give off a dim, red light, as the hydrogen gas in them is heated by radiation from nearby stars.

- **Reflection nebulae** have no light of their own.

They can only be seen because starlight shines off the dust in them.

- **The Crab nebula** is the remains of a supernova that exploded in AD1054.

- **The Great Nebula of Orion** is a glowing nebula just visible to the naked eye.

- **Dark nebulae** not only have no light of their own, they also soak up all light. They can only be seen as patches of darkness, blocking out light from the stars behind them.

- **The Horsehead nebula** in Orion is the best-known dark nebula. As its name suggests, it is shaped like a horse's head.

- **Planetary nebulae** are thin rings of gas cloud which are thrown out by dying stars. Despite their name, they have nothing to do with planets.

- **The Ring nebula** in Lyra is the best-known of the planetary nebulae.

Extraterrestrials

- **Extraterrestrial (ET)** means "outside the Earth."

- **Some scientists** say that ET life could develop anywhere in the Universe where there is a flow of energy.

- **Traces of chlorophyll**—the organic chemical vital to plant growth—may have been found on Mars.

- **Most scientists** believe that if there is ET life anywhere in the Universe, it must be based on the chemistry of carbon, as life on Earth is.

- **If civilizations like ours** exist elsewhere, they may be on planets circling other stars. This is why the discovery of other planetary systems is so exciting (see Planets).

- **The Drake Equation** was proposed by astronomer Frank Drake to work out how many civilizations there could be in our galaxy—and the figure is millions.

- **New techniques for analyzing** the atmosphere of extra-solar planets using the Hubble Space Telescope may show which of them could harbor life.

- **SETI** is the Search for Extraterrestrial Intelligence— the program that analyses radio signals from space.

- **The Arecibo radio telescope** beams out signals to distant stars.

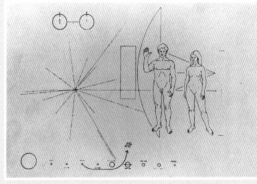

▲ The space probes Pioneer 10 and 11 carry metal panels with picture messages about life on Earth into deep space.

> ★ **STAR FACT** ★
> The life chemical formaldehyde can be detected in radio emissions from the galaxy NGC 253.

H-R diagram

- **The Hertzsprung-Russell (H-R) diagram** is a graph in which the color of stars is plotted against their brightness.

- **The color of a star** depends on its temperature.

- **Cool stars** are red or reddish-yellow.

- **Hot stars** burn white or blue.

- **Medium-sized stars** form a diagonal band called the main sequence across the graph.

- **The whiter and hotter** a main sequence star is, the brighter it shines. White stars and blue-white stars are usually bigger and younger.

- **The redder and cooler** a star is, the dimmer it glows. Cool red stars tend to be smaller and older.

- **Giant stars and white dwarf stars** lie to either side of the main sequence stars.

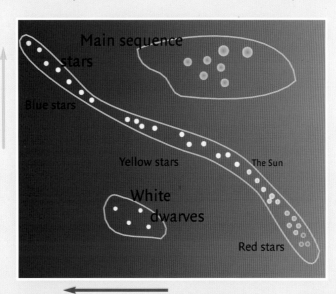

Main sequence stars

Blue stars

Yellow stars

The Sun

White dwarves

Red stars

- **The H-R diagram** shows how bright each color star should be: its absolute magnitude. If the star looks dimmer, it must be further away. By comparing a star's brightness predicted by the H-R diagram with how bright it really looks, astronomers can work out how far away it is.

- **The diagram** was first drawn up by Ejnar Hertzsprung in 1911.

The Milky Way

- **The Milky Way** is the faint, hazy band of light that you can see stretching right across the night sky.

- **Looking through binoculars**, you would see that the Milky Way is made up of countless stars.

- **A galaxy** is a vast group of stars. The Milky Way is our view of the galaxy we live in, known as the Galaxy.

- **The Milky Way Galaxy** is one of billions in space. It is made up of 100 billion stars.

- **All the stars** are arranged in a spiral with a bulge in the middle.

- **Our Sun** is just one of the billions of stars on one arm of the spiral.

- **The Galaxy** is whirling rapidly, spinning our Sun and its other stars at 62 million mph (100 million km/h).

- **The Sun** travels around the galaxy once every 200 million years—a journey of 100,000 light-years.

- **The huge bulge** at the center of the Milky Way is about 20,000 light-years across and 3,000 thick. It contains only very old stars and little dust or gas.

- **There may be a huge black hole** in the very middle of the Milky Way.

▼ *To the naked eye, the Milky Way looks like a hazy, white cloud, but binoculars show it to be a blur of countless stars.*

The Universe

- **The Universe** is everything that we can ever know—all of space and all of time.

- **The Universe** is almost entirely empty, with small clusters of matter and energy.

- **The Universe** is probably about 15 billion years old, but estimates vary.

- **There are stars** in our galaxy which are thought to be older than the estimated age of the Universe. So either the stars must be younger, or the Universe older.

- **The furthest galaxies** yet detected are about 13 billion light-years away (78 billion trillion mi/ 130 billion trillion km).

- **The Universe** is getting bigger by the second. We know this because all the galaxies are zooming away from us. The further away they are, the faster they are moving.

- **The very furthest galaxies** are spreading away from

◀ *The Universe is getting bigger and bigger all the time, as galaxies rush outward in all directions.*

us at more than 90 percent of the speed of light.

- **The Universe** was once thought to be everything that could ever exist, but recent theories about inflation (see the Big Bang) suggest our Universe may be just one of countless bubbles of space-time.

- **The Universe** may have neither a center nor an edge, because according to Einstein's theory of relativity (see Einstein), gravity bends all of space-time around into an endless curve.

> ★ **STAR FACT** ★
> Recent theories suggest there may be many other universes which we can never know.

Black holes

▲ *This is an artist's impression of what a black hole might look like, with jets of electricity shooting out from either side.*

- **Black holes** are places where gravity is so strong that it sucks everything in, including light.

- **If you fell** into a black hole you'd stretch like spaghetti.

- **Black holes form** when a star or galaxy gets so dense that it collapses under the pull of its own gravity.

- **Black holes** may exist at the heart of every galaxy.

- **Gravity shrinks** a black hole to an unimaginably small point called a singularity.

- **Around a singularity**, gravity is so intense that space-time is bent into a funnel.

- **Matter spiraling** into a black hole is torn apart and glows so brightly that it creates the brightest objects in the Universe—quasars.

- **The swirling gases** around a black hole turn it into an electrical generator, making it spout jets of electricity billions of miles out into space.

- **The opposite of black holes** may be white holes which spray out matter and light like fountains.

> ★ **STAR FACT** ★
> Black holes and white holes may join to form tunnels called wormholes, and these may be the secret to time travel.

Mercury

- **Mercury is the nearest planet** to the Sun—during its orbit it is between 28.5 and 43.3 million mi (45.9 and 69.7 million km) away.

- **Mercury is the fastest orbiting** of all the planets, getting around the Sun in just 88 days.

- **Mercury takes 58.6 days** to rotate once, so a Mercury day lasts nearly 59 times as long as ours.

- **Temperatures** on Mercury veer from −292°F (−180°C) at night to over 806°F (430°C) during the day.

- **The crust and mantle** are made largely of rock, but the core (75 percent of its diameter) is solid iron.

- **Mercury's dusty surface** is pocketed by craters made by space debris crashing into it.

- **With barely 20 percent of Earth's mass**, Mercury is so small that its gravity can only hold on to a very thin atmosphere of sodium vapor.

- **Mercury is so small** that its core has cooled and become solid (unlike Earth's). As this happened, Mercury shrank and its surface wrinkled like the skin of an old apple.

- **Craters on Mercury** discovered by the U.S.A.'s Mariner space probe have names like Bach, Beethoven, Wagner, and Shakespeare.

The largest feature on Mercury is a huge impact crater called the Caloris Basin, which is about 800mi (1,300km) across and 1.25mi (2km) deep

Most of the craters were formed by the impact of debris left over from the birth of the solar system, about four billion years ago

The surface is wrinkled by long, low ridges which probably formed as the core cooled and shrunk

▶ *Mercury is a planet of yellow dust, as deeply dented with craters as the Moon. It does have small polar icecaps, but the ice is pure acid.*

▲ *Mercury is so close to the Sun that it is not easy to see. The first time astronomers had a clear view of it was when the Mariner 10 space probe flew past it in 1974.*

Mercury's surface is covered with impact craters

Copernicus

- **Until the 16th century** most people thought the Earth was the center of the Universe and that everything—the Moon, Sun, planets, and stars— revolved around it.

- **Nicolaus Copernicus** was the astronomer who first suggested that the Sun was the center, and that the Earth went around it. This is called the heliocentric view.

- **Copernicus was born** on February 19, 1473 at Torun in Poland, and died on May 24, 1547.

- **Copernicus was the nephew** of a prince bishop who spent most of his life as a canon at Frauenberg Cathedral in East Prussia (today Germany).

- **Copernicus described his ideas** in a book called *De revolutionibus orbium coelestium* ("On the revolutions of the heavenly spheres").

- **The Roman Catholic Church** banned Copernicus's book for almost 300 years.

- **Copernicus's ideas** came not from looking at the night sky but from studying ancient astronomy.

- **Copernicus's main clue** came from the way the planets, every now and then, seem to perform a backward loop through the sky.

- **The first proof** of Copernicus's theory came in 1609, when Galileo saw (through a telescope) moons revolving around Jupiter.

- **The change in ideas** that was brought about is known as the Copernican Revolution.

▶ "The Earth," wrote Copernicus, "carrying the Moon's path, passes in a great orbit among the other planets in an annual revolution around the Sun."

Day and night

- **When it is daylight** on the half of the Earth facing toward the Sun, it is night on the half of the Earth facing away from it. As the Earth rotates, so the day and night halves shift gradually around the world.

- **The Earth turns eastward**—this means that the Sun comes up in the east as our part of the world spins around to face it.

◀ The Sun comes up to bring the dawn, as the Earth turns your part of the world around to face its light. It sets again at dusk, as the Earth goes on revolving, spinning your part of the world away from the sunlight again.

★ STAR FACT ★
One day on Venus lasts 5,832 Earth hours!

- **As the Earth turns**, the stars come back to the same place in the night sky every 23 hours, 56 minutes and 4.09 seconds. This is a sidereal day (star day).

- **It takes 24 hours** for the Sun to come back to the same place in the daytime sky. This is the solar day. It is slightly longer than the star day because the Earth moves one degree further around the Sun each day.

- **On the other planets**, the length of day and night varies according to how fast each planet rotates.

- **One day on Mercury** lasts 59 Earth days, because Mercury takes almost two months to spin around.

- **A day on Jupiter** lasts less than ten Earth hours because Jupiter spins so fast.

- **A day on Mars** is 24.6 hours—similar to ours.

- **A day on the Moon** lasts one Earth month.

Moon landings

- **The first Moon landing** was by the unmanned Soviet probe *Lunar 9*, which touched down on the Moon's surface in 1966.

- **The first men to orbit** the Moon were the astronauts on board the U.S. *Apollo 8* in 1968.

- **On July 20, 1969** the American astronauts Neil Armstrong and Edwin (Buzz) Aldrin became the first men ever to walk on the Moon.

- **When Neil Armstrong** stepped on to the Moon for the first time, he said these famous words: "That's one small step for a man; one giant leap for mankind."

- **Twelve men landed** on the Moon between 1969 and 1972.

◄ In 1969, Neil Armstrong was the first to walk on the Moon.

- **The Moon astronauts** brought back 838lb (380kg) of Moon rock.

- **A mirror was left on** the Moon's surface to reflect a laser beam which measured the Moon's distance from Earth with amazing accuracy.

- **Laser measurements** showed that, on average, the Moon is 233,806mi (376,275km) away from the Earth.

- **Gravity on the Moon** is so weak that astronauts can leap high into the air wearing their heavy space suits.

- **Temperatures** reach 243°F (117°C) at noon on the Moon, but plunge to –260°F (–162°C) at night.

Constellations

- **Constellations are patterns of stars** in the sky which astronomers use to help them pinpoint individual stars.

- **Most of the constellations** were identified long ago by the stargazers of Ancient Babylon and Egypt.

- **Constellations are simply patterns**—there is no real link between the stars whatsoever.

- **Astronomers today** recognize 88 constellations.

- **Heroes and creatures of Greek myth**, such as Orion the Hunter and Perseus, provided the names for many constellations, although each name is usually written in its Latin form, not Greek.

- **The stars in each constellation** are named after a letter of the Greek alphabet.

- **The brightest star in each constellation** is called the Alpha star, the next brightest Beta, and so on.

- **Different constellations** become visible at different times of year, as the Earth travels around the Sun.

- **Southern hemisphere constellations** are different from those in the north.

- **The constellation of the Great Bear**—also known by its Latin name Ursa Major—contains an easily recognizable group of seven stars called the Plow or the Big Dipper.

▼ Constellations are patterns of stars that help astronomers locate stars among the thousands in the night sky.

Dark matter

- **Dark matter** is space matter we cannot see because, unlike stars and galaxies, it does not give off light.

- **There is much more dark matter** in the Universe than bright. Some scientists think 90 percent is dark.

- **Astronomers know about dark matter** because its gravity pulls on stars and galaxies, changing their orbits and the way they rotate (spin around).

- **The visible stars in the Milky Way** are only a thin central slice, embedded in a big bun-shaped ball of dark matter.

- **Dark matter** is of two kinds: the matter in galaxies (galactic), and the matter between them (intergalactic).

- **Galactic dark matter** may be much the same as ordinary matter. However, it burned out (as black dwarf stars do) early in the life of the Universe.

- **Intergalactic dark matter** is made up of WIMPs (Weakly Interacting Massive Particles).

- **Some WIMPs** are called cold dark matter because they are traveling slowly away from the Big Bang.

- **Some WIMPs** are called hot dark matter because they are traveling very fast away from the Big Bang.

- **The future of the Universe** may depend on whether there is too much dark matter. If so, its gravity will eventually shrink the Universe (see the Big Bang).

▼ *A galaxy's bright stars may be only a tiny part of its total matter. Much of the galaxy may be invisible dark matter.*

Orbits

▲ *Space stations are artificial satellites that orbit the Earth. The Moon is the Earth's natural satellite.*

- **Orbit means "travel around,"** and a moon, planet, or other space object may be held within a larger space object's gravitational field and orbit it.

- **Orbits may be circular**, elliptical (oval), or parabolic (conical). The orbits of the planets are elliptical.

- **An orbiting space object** is called a satellite.

- **The biggest-known orbits** are those of the stars in the Milky Way Galaxy, which takes 200 million years.

- **Momentum** is what keeps a satellite moving through space. Its momentum depends on mass and speed.

- **A satellite orbits** at the height where its momentum exactly balances the pull of gravity.

- **If the gravitational pull** is greater than a satellite's momentum, it falls in toward the larger space object.

- **If a satellite's momentum** is greater than the pull of gravity, it flies off into space.

- **The lower a satellite orbits**, the faster it must travel to stop it from falling toward the larger space object.

- **Geostationary orbit** for one of Earth's artificial satellites is 22,236mi (35,786km) over the equator. At this height, it must travel around 685mph (11,000km/h) to complete its orbit in 24 hours. Since Earth also takes 24 hours to rotate, the satellite spins with it and so stays in the same place over the equator.

Venus

- **Venus** is the second planet out from the Sun—its orbit makes it 66 million mi (107.4 million km) away at its nearest and 67.7 million mi (109 million km) away at its furthest.

- **Venus shines like a star** in the night sky because its thick atmosphere reflects sunlight amazingly well. This planet is the brightest thing in the sky, after the Sun and the Moon.

- **Venus is called the Evening Star** because it can be seen from Earth in the evening, just after sunset. It can also be seen before sunrise, though. It is visible at these times because it is quite close to the Sun.

- **Venus's cloudy atmosphere** is a thick mixture of carbon dioxide gas and sulphuric acid, which are belched out by the planet's volcanoes.

- **Venus is the hottest planet** in the solar system, with a surface temperature of over 878°F (470°C).

- **Venus is so hot** because the carbon dioxide in its atmosphere works like the panes of glass in a greenhouse to trap the Sun's heat. This overheating

★ STAR FACT ★
Pressure on the surface of Venus is 90 times greater than that on Earth!

is called a runaway greenhouse effect.

- **Venus's thick clouds** hide its surface so well that until the Russian *Venera 13* probe landed on the planet in 1982, some people thought there might be jungles beneath the clouds.

- **Venus's day** (the time it takes to spin around once) lasts 243 Earth days—longer than its year, which lasts 224.7 days. Venus rotates backward, so the Sun comes up twice during the planet's yearly orbit.

- **Venus is the nearest** of all the planets to Earth in size, measuring 7,520mi (12,102km) across its diameter.

▼ *Venus's thick clouds of carbon dioxide gas and sulphuric acid reflect sunlight and make it shine like a star, but none of its atmosphere is transparent like the Earth's. This makes it very hard to see what is happening down on its surface.*

▲ *This is a view of a 3.7mi (6km) high volcano on Venus' surface called Maat Mons. It is not an actual photograph, but was created on computer from radar data collected by the Magellan orbiter which reached Venus in the 1980s. The colors are what astronomers guess them to be from their knowledge of the chemistry of Venus.*

Galileo

- **Galileo Galilei** (1564–1642) was a great Italian mathematician and astronomer.

- **Galileo was born** in Pisa on February 15, 1564, in the same year as William Shakespeare.

- **The pendulum clock** was invented by Galileo after watching a swinging lamp in Pisa Cathedral in 1583.

- **Galileo's experiments** with balls rolling down slopes laid the basis for our understanding of how gravity makes things accelerate (speed up).

- **Learning of the telescope's invention**, Galileo made his own to look at the Moon, Venus, and Jupiter.

> ★ **STAR FACT** ★
> Only on October 13, 1992 was the sentence of the Catholic Church on Galileo retracted.

◄ *One of the most brilliant of scientists of all time, Galileo ended his life imprisoned (in his villa near Florence) for his beliefs.*

- **Galileo described his observations** of space in a book called *The Starry Messenger*, published in 1613.

- **Through his telescope** Galileo saw that Jupiter has four moons (see Jupiter's Galilean moons). He also saw that Venus has phases (as our Moon does).

- **Jupiter's moon and Venus's phases** were the first visible evidence of Copernicus' theory that the Earth moves round the Sun. Galileo also believed this.

- **Galileo was declared a heretic** in 1616 by the Catholic Church, for his support of Copernican theory. Later, threatened with torture, Galileo was forced to deny that the Earth orbits the Sun. Legend has it he muttered *"eppur si muove"* ("yet it does move") afterward.

Earth's formation

▲ *Earth and the Solar System formed from a cloud of gas and dust.*

- **The Solar System** was created when the gas cloud left over from a giant supernova explosion started to collapse in on itself and spin.

- **About 4.55 billion years ago** there was just a vast, hot cloud of dust and gas circling a new star, our Sun.

- **The Earth probably began** when tiny pieces of space debris (called planetesimals) began to clump together, pulled together by each other's gravity.

- **As the Earth formed**, more space debris kept on smashing into it, adding new material. This debris included ice from the edges of the solar system.

- **About 4.5 billion years ago**, a rock the size of Mars crashed into the Earth. The splashes of material from this crash clumped together to form the Moon.

- **The collision** that formed the Moon made the Earth very hot.

- **Radioactive decay** heated the Earth even further.

- **For a long time** the surface of the Earth was a mass of erupting volcanoes.

- **Iron and nickel melted** and sank to form the core.

- **Lighter materials** such as aluminum, oxygen, and silicon floated up and cooled to form the crust.

Distances

- **The distance to the Moon** is measured with a laser beam.

- **The distance to the planets** is measured by bouncing radar signals off them and timing how long the signals take to get there and back.

- **The distance to nearby stars** is worked out by measuring the slight shift in the angle of each star in comparison to stars far away, as the Earth orbits the Sun. This is called parallax shift.

- **Parallax shift** can only be used to measure nearby stars, so astronomers work out the distance to faraway stars and galaxies by comparing how bright they look with how bright they actually are.

- **For middle distance stars**, astronomers compare color with brightness using the Hertzsprung-Russell (H-R) diagram. This is called main sequence fitting.

◀ *Estimating the distance to the stars is one of the major problems in astronomy.*

- **Beyond 30,000 light-years**, stars are too faint for main sequence fitting to work.

- **Distances to nearby galaxies** can be estimated using "standard candles" —stars whose brightness astronomers know, such as Cepheid variables (see Variable stars), supergiants, and supernovae.

- **The expected brightness of a galaxy** too far away to pick out its stars may be worked out using the Tully-Fisher technique, based on how fast galaxies spin.

- **Counting planetary nebulae** (the rings of gas left behind by supernova explosions) is another way of working out how bright a distant galaxy should be.

- **A third method** of calculating the brightness of a distant galaxy is to gauge how mottled it looks.

Spacecraft

- **There are three kinds of spacecraft:** artificial satellites, unmanned probes, and manned spacecraft.

- **Spacecraft** have double hulls (outer coverings) to protect against other space objects that crash into them.

- **Manned spacecraft** must also protect the crew from heat and other dangerous effects of launch and landing.

- **Spacecraft windows** have filters to protect astronauts from the Sun's dangerous ultraviolet rays.

- **Radiators** outside of the spacecraft lose heat to stop the crew's temperatures from overheating the craft.

- **Manned spacecraft** have life-support systems that provide oxygen to breathe, usually mixed with nitrogen (as in ordinary air). Charcoal filters out smells.

- **The carbon dioxide** crews breathe out is absorbed by pellets of lithium hydroxide.

- **Spacecraft toilets** have to get rid of waste in low gravity conditions. Astronauts have to sit on a device which sucks away the waste. Solid waste is dried and dumped in space, but the water is saved.

- **To wash,** astronauts have a waterproof shower which sprays them with jets of water from all sides and also sucks away all the waste water.

★ **STAR FACT** ★
The weightlessness of space means that most astronauts sleep floating in the air, held in place by a few straps.

▶ *The U.S. space shuttle, the first reusable spacecraft, has made manned space flights out into Earth's orbit and back almost a matter of routine.*

The Earth

- **The Earth is the third planet** out from the Sun, 90 million mi (149.6 million km) away on average. On January 3, at the nearest point of its orbit (called the perihelion), the Earth is 91,404,830mi (147,097,800km) away from the Sun. On July 4, at its furthest (the aphelion), it is 94,513,020mi (152,098,200km) away.

- **The Earth is the fifth largest planet** in the solar system, with a diameter of 12,756mi (7,926km) and a circumference of 24,870mi (40,024km) at the Equator.

- **The Earth is one of four rocky planets**, along with Mercury, Venus, and Mars. It is made mostly of rock, with a core of iron and nickel.

- **No other planet in the solar system** has liquid on its surface, which is why Earth is uniquely suitable for life. Over 70 percent of Earth's surface is under water.

- **The Earth's atmosphere** is mainly harmless nitrogen and life-giving oxygen, and it is over 435mi (700km) deep. The oxygen has been made and maintained by plants over billions of years.

- **The Earth formed 4.65 billion years ago** from clouds of space dust whirling around the young Sun. The planet was so hot that it was molten at first. Only slowly did the surface cool into a hard crust.

- **The Earth's orbit** around the Sun is 584,018,332mi (939,886,400km) long and takes 365.242 days.

- **The Earth is tilted** at an angle of 23.5°. Even so, it orbits the Sun in a level plane, called the plane of the ecliptic.

- **The Earth is made up** of the same basic materials as the other rocky planets—mostly iron (35 percent), oxygen (28 percent), magnesium (17 percent), silicon (13 percent), and nickel (2.7 percent).

> ★ **STAR FACT** ★
> The Earth is protected from the Sun's radiation by a magnetic field which stretches 37,282mi (60,000km) out into space.

▼ The Earth looks mostly bright blue from space—this is due to the unique presence of water on its surface.

▲ Most of the Earth's rocky crust is drowned beneath oceans, formed from steam belched out by volcanoes early in the planet's history. The Earth is just the right distance from the Sun for surface temperatures to stay an average 59°F (15°C), and keep most of its water liquid.

Comets

▲ *Comet Kahoutek streaks through the night sky.*

- **Comets are bright objects** with long tails, which we sometimes see streaking across the night sky.

- **They may look spectacular**, but a comet is just a dirty ball of ice a mile or so across.

- **Many comets orbit the Sun**, but their orbits are very long and they spend most of the time in the far

reaches of the solar system. We see them when their orbit brings them close to the Sun for a few weeks.

- **A comet's tail** is made as it nears the Sun and begins to melt. A vast plume of gas millions of miles across is blown out behind by the solar wind. The tail is what you see, shining as the sunlight catches it.

- **Comets called periodics** appear at regular intervals.

- **Some comets reach speeds** of 1.25 million mph (2 million km/h) as they near the Sun.

- **Far away from the Sun**, comets slow down to 600 mph (1,000km/h) or so—that is why they stay away for so long.

- **The visit of the comet Hale-Bopp** in 1997 gave the brightest view of a comet since 1811, visible even from brightly lit cities.

- **The Shoemaker-Levy 9 comet** smashed into Jupiter in July 1994, with the biggest crash ever witnessed.

- **The most famous comet** of all is Halley's comet.

Giant stars

- **Giant stars** are 10 to 100 times as big as the Sun, and 10 to 1,000 times as bright.

- **Red giants** are stars that have swollen 10 to 100 times their size, as they reach the last stages of their life and their outer gas layers cool and expand.

- **Giant stars have burned** all their hydrogen, and so burn helium, fusing (joining) helium atoms to make carbon.

- **The biggest stars** go on swelling after they become red giants, and grow into supergiants.

- **Supergiant stars** are up to 500 times as big as the Sun, with absolute magnitudes of –5 to –10 (see Star brightness).

- **Pressure in the heart** of a supergiant is enough to

fuse carbon atoms together to make iron.

- **All the iron in the Universe** was made in the heart of supergiant stars.

- **There is a limit to the brightness** of supergiants, so they can be used as distance markers by comparing how bright they look to how bright they are (see Distances).

- **Supergiant stars** eventually collapse and explode as supernovae.

▶ The constellation of Cygnus, the Swan, contains the very biggest star in the known Universe—a hypergiant which is almost a million times as big as the Sun.

> ★ **STAR FACT** ★
> The biggest-known star is the hypergiant Cygnus OB2 No.12, which is 810,000 times as bright as the Sun.

Eclipses

- **An eclipse** is when the light from a star such as the Sun is temporarily blocked off by another space object.

- **A lunar eclipse** is when the Moon travels behind the Earth, and into the Earth's shadow (Earth is between the Moon and the Sun).

- **Lunar eclipses happen once or twice** every year and last only a few hours.

- **In a total lunar eclipse**, the Moon turns rust red.

- **There will be a lunar eclipses** on May 16 and November 9, 2003 and on May 4, and October 28, 2004.

- **A solar eclipse** is when the Moon comes between the Sun and the Earth, casting a shadow a couple of miles wide on to the Earth's surface.

- **In a total eclipse of the Sun**, the Moon passes directly in front of the Sun, completely covering it so that only its corona can be seen (see the Sun).

- **There are one or two solar eclipses every year**, but they are visible only from a narrow strip of the world.

▲ During a total solar eclipse of the Sun, the Moon blocks out everything but the Sun's corona.

- **There will be a total solar eclipse** on November 23, 2003, visible from Antarctica.

- **Solar eclipses are possible** because the Moon is 400 times smaller than the Sun, and is also 400 times closer to the Earth. This means the Sun and the Moon appear to be the same size in the sky.

Star brightness

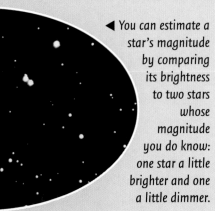

◄ You can estimate a star's magnitude by comparing its brightness to two stars whose magnitude you do know: one star a little brighter and one a little dimmer.

- **Star brightness** is worked out on a scale of magnitude (amount) that was first devised in 150BC by the Ancient Greek astronomer Hipparchus.

- **The brightest star** Hipparchus could see was Antares, and he described it as magnitude 1. He described the faintest star he could see as magnitude 6.

- **Using telescopes and binoculars**, astronomers can now see much fainter stars than Hipparchus could.

- **Good binoculars** show magnitude 9 stars, while a home telescope will show magnitude 10 stars.

- **Brighter stars than Antares** have been identified with magnitudes of less than 1, and even minus numbers. Betelgeuse is 0.8, Vega is 0.0, and the Sun is −26.7.

- **The brightest-looking star** from Earth is Sirius, the Dog Star, with a magnitude of −1.4.

- **The magnitude scale only** describes how bright a star looks from Earth compared to other stars. This is its relative magnitude.

- **The further away a star is,** the dimmer it looks and the smaller its relative magnitude is, regardless of how bright it really is.

- **A star's absolute magnitude** describes how bright a star really is.

- **The star Deneb** is 60,000 times brighter than the Sun. But because it is 1,800 light-years away, it looks dimmer than Sirius.

Herschel

- **William Herschel** (1738–1822) was an amateur astronomer who built his own, very powerful telescope in his home in Bath, England.

- **Until Herschel's time**, astronomers assumed there were just seven independent objects in the sky: the Moon, the Sun, and five planets.

- **The five known planets** were Mercury, Venus, Mars, Jupiter, and Saturn.

- **Uranus**, the sixth planet, was discovered by William Herschel in 1781.

- **At first, Herschel** had thought that the dot of light he could see through his telescope was a star. But when he looked more closely, he saw a tiny disk instead of a point of light. When he looked the next night, the "star" had moved—this meant that it had to be a planet.

◀ William Herschel was one of the greatest astronomers. With the help of his sister Caroline, he discovered Uranus in 1781. He later identified two of the moons of Uranus and Saturn.

- **Herschel wanted to name** the planet George, after King George III, but Uranus was eventually chosen.

- **Herschel's partner** in his discoveries was his sister Caroline (1750–1848), another great astronomer, who cataloged (listed) all the stars of the northern hemisphere.

- **Herschel's son John** cataloged the stars of the southern hemisphere.

- **Herschel himself added** to the catalog of nebulae.

- **Herschel was also the first** to explain that the Milky Way is our view of a galaxy shaped "like a grindstone."

Rockets

- **Rockets** provide the huge thrust needed to beat the pull of Earth's gravity and launch a spacecraft into space.

- **Rockets burn propellant** (propel means "push"), to produce hot gases that drive the rocket upward.

- **Rocket propellant** comes in two parts: a solid or liquid fuel, and an oxidizer.

- **Solid fuel** is a rubbery substance that contains hydrogen, and it is usually used in additional, booster rockets.

- **Liquid fuel** is usually liquid hydrogen, and it is typically used on big rockets.

- **There is no oxygen in space**, and the oxidizer supplies the oxygen needed to burn fuel. It is usually liquid oxygen (called "lox" for short).

- **The first rockets** were made 1,000 years ago in China.

- **Robert Goddard** launched the very first liquid-fuel rocket in 1926.

- **The German V2 war rocket**, designed by Werner von Braun, was the first rocket capable of reaching space.

▶ Unlike other spacecraft, the space shuttle can land like an airplane ready for another mission. But even the shuttle has to be launched into space on the back of huge rockets. These soon fall back to Earth where they are gathered for reuse.

> ★ STAR FACT ★
> The most powerful rocket ever was the *Saturn 5*
> that sent astronauts to the Moon.

Satellites

- **Satellites are objects** that orbit planets and other space objects. Moons are natural satellites. Spacecraft sent up to orbit the Earth and the Sun are artificial satellites.

- **The first artificial satellite** was *Sputnik 1*, launched on October 4, 1957.

- **Over 100 artificial satellites** are now launched every year. A few of them are space telescopes.

- **Communications satellites** beam everything from TV pictures to telephone calls around the world.

- **Observation satellites** scan the Earth and are used for purposes such as scientific research, weather forecasting, and spying.

- **Navigation satellites** such as the Global Positioning System (GPS) are used by people such as airline pilots to figure out exactly where they are.

- **Satellites are launched** at a particular speed and trajectory (path) to place them in just the right orbit.

- **The lower a satellite's orbit**, the faster it must fly to avoid falling back to Earth. Most satellites fly in low orbits, 300mi (500km) above the Earth.

- **A geostationary orbit** is 22,236mi (35,786km) up. Satellites in geostationary orbit over the Equator always stay in exactly the same place above the Earth.

- **Polar orbiting satellites** circle the Earth from pole to pole about 530mi (850mi) up, covering a different strip of the Earth's surface on each orbit.

▼ *One of the many hundreds of satellites now in Earth's orbit.*

Hipparchus

▲ *Some of Hipparchus' knowledge of the stars came from the Sumerians who wrote a lot of their findings on clay tablets*

- **Hipparchus of Nicaea** was a Greek astronomer who lived in the 2nd century BC, dying in 127BC.

- **Hipparchus created** the basic framework of astronomy. This was developed into a system that lasted 1,500 years, until they were overthrown by the ideas of Copernicus.

- **Ancient Babylonian records** brought back by Alexander the Great from his conquests helped Hipparchus to make his observations of the stars.

- **Hipparchus was the first astronomer** to try to figure out how far away the Sun is.

- **The first star catalog**, listing 850 stars, was put together by Hipparchus.

- **Hipparchus was also the first** to identify the constellations systematically and to assess stars in terms of magnitude (see star brightness).

- **Hipparchus also discovered** that the relative positions of the stars on the equinoxes (March 21 and December 21) shift round, taking 26,000 years to return. This is called the "procession of the equinoxes."

- **The mathematics of trigonometry** is also thought to have been invented by Hipparchus.

- **Hipparchus** measured the year to within an incredibly accurate 6.5 minutes.

Mars

- **Mars** is the nearest planet to Earth after Venus, and it is the only planet to have either an atmosphere or a daytime temperature close to ours.

- **Mars is called the red planet** because of its rusty red color. This comes from oxidized (rusted) iron in its soil.

- **Mars is the fourth planet** out from the Sun, orbiting it at an average distance of 141.6 million mi. It takes 687 days to complete its orbit.

- **Mars is 4,217mi (6,786km)** in diameter and spins around once every 24.62 hours—almost the same time as the Earth takes to rotate.

- **Mars's volcano Olympus Mons** is the biggest in the solar system. It covers the same area as Ireland and is three times higher than Mount Everest.

- **In the 1880s**, the American astronomer Percival Lowell was convinced that the dark lines he could see on Mars's surface through his telescope were canals built by Martians.

> ★ STAR FACT ★
> The 1997 Mars Pathfinder mission showed that many of the rocks on Mars's surface were dumped in their positions by a huge flood at least two billion years ago.

- **The Viking probes** found no evidence of life on Mars, but the discovery of a possible fossil of a microorganism in a Mars rock (see Life) means the hunt for life on Mars is on. Future missions to the planet will hunt for life below its surface.

- **The evidence is growing** that Mars was warmer and wetter in the past, although scientists cannot say how much water there was, or when and why it dried up.

- **Mars has two tiny moons** called Phobos and Deimos. Phobos is just 17mi (27km) across, while Deimos is just 9.3mi (15km) across and has so little gravity that you could reach escape velocity (see Take off) riding a bike up a ramp!

▼ Mars's surface is cracked by a valley called the Vallis Marineris—so big it makes the Grand Canyon look tiny.

Vallis Marineris

Ascraeus Mons volcano

Pavonis Mons volcano

Arsia Mons volcano

Polar icecap

▶ Mars is the best known planet besides Earth, studied by countless astronomers through powerful telescopes, scanned by orbiting space probes, and landed on more times than any other planet. All this effort has revealed a planet with a surface like a red, rocky desert, but there is also plenty of evidence that Mars wasn't always so desert-like.

Light

- **Light is the fastest thing** in the Universe, traveling at 186,000mi/sec (299,792,458m/sec).

- **Light rays always travel** in straight lines.

- **Light rays change direction** as they pass from one material to another. This is called refraction.

- **Colors** are different wavelengths of light.

- **The longest light waves** you can see are red, and the shortest are violet.

- **Light is a form** of electromagnetic radiation (see Magnetism and radiation), and a light ray is a stream of tiny energy particles called photons.

- **Photons of light** travel in waves just 380 to 750 nanometers (millionths of a millimeter) long.

- **Faint light** from very distant stars is often recorded by sensors called CCDs (see Observatories). These count photons from the star as they arrive and build up a picture of the star bit by bit over a long period.

- **The electromagnetic spectrum** (range) includes ultraviolet light and X-rays, but light is the only part of the spectrum our eyes can see.

- **All light is given out by atoms**, and atoms give out light when they are "excited," for example, in a nuclear reaction.

▼ *Stars send out huge amounts of light and other radiation as they are heated within by stupendously big nuclear reactions.*

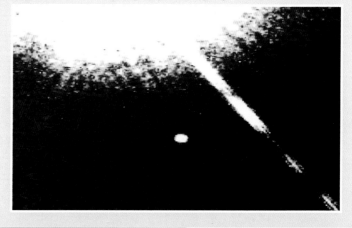

Magnetism

- **Magnetism is a force** that either pulls magnetic materials together or pushes them apart.

- **Iron and nickel** are the most common magnetic materials. Electricity is also magnetic.

- **Around every magnet** there is a region in which its effects are felt, called its magnetic field.

- **The magnetic field** around a planet or a star is called the magnetosphere.

◄ *The planet Jupiter is one of the most powerful magnets in the Solar System. It was first detected by "synchrotron radiation"—the radiation from tiny electrons accelerating as they fall into a magnetic field.*

- **Most of the planets** in the Solar System, including the Earth, have a magnetic field.

- **Planets have magnetic fields** because of the liquid iron in their cores. As the planets rotate, so the iron swirls, generating electric currents that create the magnetic field.

- **Jupiter's magnetic field** is 30 times stronger than that of the Earth, because Jupiter is huge and spins very quickly.

- **Neptune and Uranus** are unusual because, unlike other planets' magnetic fields, theirs are at right angles to their axis of rotation (the angle at which they spin).

- **Magnetism is linked** to electricity, and together they make up the force called electromagnetism.

- **Electromagnetism** is one of the four fundamental forces in the Universe, along with gravity and the two basic forces of the atomic nucleus.

Atmosphere

- **An atmosphere** is the gases held around a planet by its gravity.

- **Every planet in the Solar System** has an atmosphere.

- **Each atmosphere** is very different. Earth's atmosphere is the only one humans can breathe.

- **Atmospheres** are not fixed, but can change rapidly.

▼ *Earth's unique atmosphere shields us from the Sun's dangerous rays, as well as giving us oxygen and water.*

★ STAR FACT ★
The oxygen in Earth's atmosphere was formed entirely by microscopic plants.

- **Moons** are generally too small and their gravity is too weak to hold on to an atmosphere. But some moons in the solar system have one, including Saturn's moon Titan.

- **The primordial (earliest) atmospheres** came from the swirling cloud of gas and dust surrounding the young Sun.

- **If Earth and the other rocky planets** had primordial atmospheres, they were stripped away by the solar wind (see Solar eruptions).

- **Earth's atmosphere** was formed first from gases pouring out of volcanoes.

- **Jupiter's atmosphere** is partly primordial, but it has been altered by the Sun's radiation, and the planet's own internal heat and lightning storms.

Cosmic rays

- **Cosmic rays** are streams of high-energy particles that strike Earth's atmosphere.

- **The lowest-energy cosmic rays** come from the Sun, or are Galactic Cosmic Rays (GCRs) from outside the Solar System.

- **Medium-energy cosmic rays** come from sources within our own Milky Way, including powerful supernova explosions.

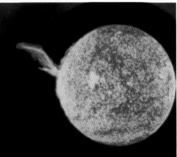

- **Collisions** between cosmic rays and the hydrogen gas clouds left by supernovae create a kind of radiation called synchrotron radiation, which can be picked up from places such as the Crab nebula by radio telescopes.

- **The highest-energy cosmic rays** may come from outside our galaxy.

- **About 85 percent of GCRs** are the nuclei of hydrogen atoms, stripped of their electron (see Atoms).

◄ *Because Earth's magnetic field makes cosmic rays spiral into our atmosphere, it is not always easy to identify where they have come from. However, many are from the surface of the Sun.*

- **Most other GCRs** are helium and heavier nuclei, but there are also tiny positrons, electrons and neutrinos.

- **Neutrinos** are so small that they pass almost straight through the Earth without stopping.

- **The study of cosmic rays** provided scientists with most of their early knowledge about high-energy particles—every subatomic particle apart from electrons, protons, and neutrons.

- **Most cosmic rays** are deflected (pushed aside) by the Earth's magnetic field or collide with particles in the atmosphere long before they reach the ground.

Jupiter

- **Jupiter** is the biggest planet in the Solar System—twice as heavy as all the other planets put together.

- **Jupiter has no surface** for a spacecraft to land on because it is made mostly from helium gas and hydrogen. The massive pull of Jupiter's gravity squeezes the hydrogen so hard that it is liquid.

- **Toward Jupiter's core**, immense pressure turns the hydrogen to solid metal.

- **The Ancient Greeks** originally named the planet Zeus, after the king of their gods. Jupiter was the Romans' name for Zeus.

- **Jupiter spins right around** in less than ten hours, which means that the planet's surface is moving at nearly 31,000mph (50,000km/h).

Great Red Spot

! NEWS FLASH !
The Galileo space probe is soon to end its ten year exploration of Jupiter and its moons.

- **Jupiter's speedy spin makes** its middle bulge out. It also churns up the planet's metal core until it generates a hugely powerful magnetic field (see Magnetism), ten times as strong as the Earth's.

- **Jupiter has a Great Red Spot**—a huge swirl of red clouds measuring more than 25,000mi (40,000km) across. The scientist Robert Hooke first noticed the spot in 1644.

- **Jupiter's four biggest moons** were first spotted by Galileo in the 17th century (see Jupiter's Galilean moons). Their names are Io, Europa, Callisto, and Ganymede.

- **Jupiter also has 17 smaller moons:** Metis, Adastrea, Amalthea, Thebe, Leda, Himalia, Lysithea, Elara, Ananke, Carme, Pasiphaë, Sinope, as well as five recent discoveries.

- **Jupiter is so massive** that the pressure at its heart makes it glow very faintly with invisible infrared rays. Indeed, it glows as brightly as four million billion 100-watt light bulbs. But it is not quite big enough for nuclear reactions to start, and make it become a star.

◀ *Jupiter is a gigantic planet, 88,846mi (142,953km) across. Its orbit takes 11.86 years and varies between 460 and 506 million mi (740.9 and 815.7 million km) from the Sun. Its surface is often rent by huge lightning flashes and thunderclaps, and temperatures here plunge to −238°F (−150°C). Looking at Jupiter's surface, all you can see is a swirling mass of red, brown, and yellow clouds of ammonia, including the Great Red Spot.*

Space probes

- **Space probes** are automatic, computer-controlled unmanned spacecraft sent out to explore space.

- **The first successful** planetary probe was the U.S.A.'s *Mariner 2*, which flew past Venus in 1962.

- *Mariner 10* reached Mercury in 1974.

- *Vikings 1* and *2* **landed** on Mars in 1976.

- *Voyager 2* has flown over 3.7 billion mi (6 billion km) and is heading out of the Solar System. It passed close to Jupiter (1979), Saturn (1980), Uranus (1986), and Neptune (1989).

- **Most probes** are "fly-bys" which spend just a few days passing their target and beaming back data to Earth.

- **To save fuel** on journeys to distant planets, space probes may use a nearby planet's gravity to catapult them on their way. This is called a slingshot.

> **! NEWS FLASH !**
> NASA' s Terrestrial Planet Finder (TPF) may set off to visit planets circling nearby stars in 2009.

- **In the next decade**, more than 50 space probes will be sent off to visit planets, asteroids, and comets, as well as to observe the Moon and the Sun.

- **Space probes** will bring back samples from Mars, comets, and asteroids in the next few years.

▼ *Probes are equipped with a wealth of equipment for recording data and beaming it back to Earth.*

Hubble

▲ *One of Hubble's earliest achievements was to show that some "nebulae" were really other galaxies.*

- **Edwin Hubble** (1889–1953) was an American who trained in law at Chicago and Oxford, and was also a great boxer before he turned to astronomy.

- **Until the early 20th century**, astronomers thought that our galaxy was all there was to the Universe.

- **In the 1920s Hubble** showed that the fuzzy patches of light once thought to be nebulae were in fact other galaxies far beyond the Milky Way.

- **In 1929 Hubble** measured the red shift of 18 galaxies, and showed that they were all moving away from us.

- **Red shift showed Hubble** that the further away a galaxy is, the faster it is moving.

- **The ratio of a galaxy's distance** to the speed it is moving away from us is now known as Hubble's Law.

- **Hubble's Law** showed that the Universe is getting bigger, and so must have started very small. This led to the idea of the Big Bang.

- **The figure given** by Hubble's law is Hubble's constant. About 25 to 50 mi/sec (40 to 80 km/sec) per megaparsec.

- **In the 1930s Hubble** showed that the Universe is isotropic (the same in all directions).

- **Hubble space telescope** is named after Edwin Hubble.

Meteors

▲ This crater in Arizona is one of the few large meteorite crater's visible on Earth. The Moon is covered in them.

- **Meteors** are space objects that crash into Earth's atmosphere. They may be stray asteroids, tiny meteoroids, or the grains of dust from the tails of dying comets.
- **Meteoroids** are the billions of tiny lumps of rocky material that hurtle around the solar system. Most are no bigger than a pea.

- **Most meteors** are very small and burn up as they enter the atmosphere.
- **Shooting stars** are actually meteors burning up as they hit Earth's atmosphere.
- **Meteor showers** are bursts of dozens of shooting stars which arrive as Earth hits the tail of a comet.
- **Although meteors are not stars**, meteor showers are named after the constellations they seem to come from.
- **The heaviest showers** are the Perseids (August 12), the Geminids (December 13), and the Quadrantids (January 3).
- **Meteorites** are larger meteors that penetrate right through Earth's atmosphere and reach the ground.
- **A large meteorite** could hit the Earth at any time.

> ★ STAR FACT ★
> The impact of a large meteorite may have chilled the Earth and wiped out the dinosaurs.

Pulsars

- **A pulsar** is a neutron star that spins rapidly, beaming out regular pulses of radio waves—kind of like an invisible cosmic lighthouse.
- **The first pulsar** was detected by a Cambridge astronomer called Jocelyn Bell Burnell in 1967.

▶ The Crab nebula contains a pulsar also known as NP0532. It is the youngest pulsar yet discovered and it probably formed after the supernova explosion seen in the Crab nebula in AD1054. It has a rotation period of 0.0331 seconds, but it is gradually slowing down.

- **At first astronomers thought** the regular pulses might be signals from aliens, and pulsars were jokingly called LGMs (short for Little Green Men).
- **Most pulsars** send their radio pulse about once a second. The slowest pulse only every four seconds, and the fastest every 1.6 milliseconds.
- **The pulse rate** of a pulsar slows down as it gets older.
- **The Crab pulsar** slows by a millionth each day.
- **More than 650 pulsars** are now known, but there may be 100,000 active in our galaxy.
- **Pulsars probably result** from a supernova explosion—that is why most are found in the flat disk of the Milky Way, where supernovae occur.
- **Pulsars are not found** in the same place as supernovae because they form after the debris from the explosion has spread into space.
- **We know** they come from tiny neutron stars often less than 6mi (10km) across, as they pulse so fast.

Elements

- **Elements** are the basic chemicals of the Universe. There are no simpler substances, and they cannot be broken down into other substances.

- **Elements are formed** entirely of atoms that contain the same number of protons in their nuclei (see Atoms). All hydrogen atoms have one proton, for instance.

- **More than 100 elements** are known.

- **The simplest and lightest elements**—hydrogen and helium—formed very early in the history of the Universe (see the Big Bang).

- **Other elements** formed as the nuclei of the atoms of the light elements joined in a process called nuclear fusion.

- **Nuclear fusion of element atoms** happens deep inside stars because of the pressure of their gravity.

> ★ STAR FACT ★
> Massive atoms like uranium and thorium are formed by the shock waves from supernovae.

- **Lighter elements** like oxygen and carbon formed first.

- **Helium nuclei** fused with oxygen and neon atoms to form atoms like silicon, magnesium, and calcium.

- **Heavy atoms** like iron formed when massive supergiant stars neared the end of their life and collapsed, boosting the pressure of the gravity in their core hugely. Even now iron is forming inside dying supergiants.

▶ Nebulae like this one, Orion, contain many elements. Some (such as oxygen, silicon, and carbon) formed in their stars, but their hydrogen and helium formed in deep space very long ago.

Kepler

▶ Despite almost losing his eyesight and the use of his hands through smallpox at the age of three, Johannes Kepler became an assistant to the great Danish astronomer Tycho Brahe, and took over his work when Brahe died.

- **Johannes Kepler** (1571–1630) was the German astronomer who discovered the basic rules about the way the planets move.

- **Kepler got his ideas** from studying Mars' movement.

- **Before Kepler's discoveries**, people thought that the planets moved in circles.

- **Kepler discovered** that the true shape of the planets' orbits is elliptical (oval). This is Kepler's first law.

- **Kepler's second law** is that the speed of a planet through space varies with its distance from the Sun.

- **A planet moves fastest** when its orbit brings it nearest to the Sun (called its perihelion). It moves slowest when it is farthest from the Sun (called its aphelion).

- **Kepler's third law** is that a planet's period—the time it takes to complete its yearly orbit of the Sun—depends on its distance from the Sun.

- **Kepler's third law states** that the square of a planet's period is proportional to the cube of its average distance from the Sun.

- **Kepler believed** that the planets made harmonious music as they moved—"the music of the spheres."

- **Kepler also wrote a book** about measuring how much wine there was in wine casks, which proved to be important for the mathematics of calculus.

Space shuttle

- **The space shuttle** is a reusable spacecraft, made up of a 122ft (37m) long orbiter, two big Solid Rocket Boosters (SRBs), three main engines, and a tank.

- **The shuttle orbiter is launched** into space on the SRBs, which fall away to be picked up for reuse.

- **The orbiter can only go** as high as a near-Earth orbit, some 185mi (300km) above the Earth.

- **The maximum crew** is eight, and a basic mission is seven days, during which the crew work in shirtsleeves.

- **Orbiter toilets** use flowing air to suck away waste.

- **The orbiter can carry** a 55,115lb (25,000kg) load in its cargo bay.

- **The first four orbiters** were named after old sailing ships: *Columbia, Challenger, Discovery,* and *Atlantis.*

- **Three engines** are used only for lift off. In space, the small Orbital Maneuvering System (OMS) engines take over. The Reaction Control System (RCS) makes small adjustments to the orbiter's position.

- **The shuttle program** was brought to a temporary halt in 1986, when the *Challenger* exploded shortly after launch, killing its crew of seven.

- **In 1994 the crew of *Discovery*** repaired the Hubble space telescope in orbit.

▲ *The entire center section of the orbiter is a cargo bay which can be opened in space so satellites can be placed in orbit.*

Moons

▼ *Saturn's moon Enceladus is marked by deep valleys, suggesting geological activity. This is quite rare in moons and smaller planets.*

- **Moons** are the natural satellites of planets. Most are small rock globes that continually orbit the parent planet, held in place by the planet's gravity.

- **There are 65 known** moons in the Solar System.

- **Every planet in the Solar System** has a moon, apart from Mercury and Venus, the nearest planets to the Sun.

- **New moons are frequently discovered**, as space probes such as the *Voyagers* reach distant planets.

- **Three moons** have atmospheres: Saturn's moon Titan, Jupiter's Io, and Neptune's Triton.

- **The largest moon** in the Solar System is Jupiter's moon Ganymede.

- **The second largest** is Saturn's moon Titan. This moon is rather like a small frozen Earth, with a rocky core beneath a cold, nitrogen atmosphere.

- **The smallest moons** are rocky lumps just a few miles across, rather like asteroids.

- **Saturn's moon Iapetus** is white on one side and black on the other.

- **Saturn's moon Enceladus** is only 310mi (500km) across, and glistens because it is covered in beads of ice.

Saturn

- **Saturn is the second biggest planet** in the Solar System—815 times as big in volume as the Earth, and measuring 74,565mi (20,000km) around its equator.

- **Saturn takes 29.5 years** to travel around the Sun, so Saturn's year is 29.46 Earth years. The planet's complete orbit is a journey of more than 2.8 billion mi (4.5 billion km).

- **Winds ten times stronger than** a hurricane on Earth swirl around Saturn's equator, reaching up to 683mph (1,100km/h)—and they never let up.

- **Saturn is named after Saturnus**, the Ancient Roman god of seed-time and harvest. He was celebrated in the Roman's wild, Christmas-time festival of Saturnalia.

- **Because Saturn is so massive**, the pressure at its heart is enough to turn hydrogen solid. That is why there is a layer of metallic hydrogen around the planet's inner core of rock.

- **Saturn is not solid**, but is made almost entirely of gas, mostly liquid hydrogen and helium. Only in the

★ STAR FACT ★
Saturn is so low in density that if you found a bathtub big enough, you would be able to float the planet in the water.

planet's very small core is there any solid rock.

- **Saturn is one of the fastest spinning** of all the planets. Despite its size, it rotates in just 11.5 hours, which means it turns around at over 6,215mph (10,000km/h).

- **Saturn's surface appears** to be almost completely smooth, though *Voyager 1* and *2* did photograph a few small, swirling storms when they flew past.

- **Saturn has a very powerful magnetic field** (see Magnetism) and sends out strong radio signals.

Saturn's rings are made of many millions of tiny, ice-coated rock fragments

◀ Saturn is the queen of the planets. Almost as big as Jupiter, and made largely of liquid hydrogen and helium, Saturn is stunningly beautiful, with its smooth, pale-butterscotch surface (clouds of ammonia) and its shimmering halo of rings. But it is a very secretive planet. Telescopes have never pierced its upper atmosphere, and data from the fly-bys of the Voyager probes focused on its rings and moons. But the Cassini probe, launched in 1997, may change this when it eventually descends into Saturn's atmosphere.

Space stations

- **The first space station** was the Soviet *Salyut 1* launched in April 1971. Its low orbit meant it stayed up only five months.

- **The first U.S. space station** was *Skylab*. Three crews spent 171 days in it in 1973–74.

- **The longest serving station** was the Soviet *Mir*— launched in 1986, it made more than 76,000 orbits of the Earth. The last crew left in late 1999.

- *Mir* **was built in stages.** It weighed 125 tons and had six docking ports and two living rooms, plus a bathroom and two small individual cabins.

- **There is neither an up nor a down** in a space station, but *Mir* had carpets on the "floor," pictures on the "wall," and lights on the "ceiling."

> **! NEWS FLASH !**
> The living space on the ISS will be bigger than the passenger space on two jumbo jets.

- **The giant International Space Station (ISS)** is being built in stages and should be complete in 2004.

- **The first crew** went aboard the ISS in January 2000.

- **The ISS** will be 355ft (108m) long and 295ft (90m) wide, and weigh 450 tons.

- **In April 2001**, Californian Dennis Tito became the first ever space tourist.

▶ Mir *space station, photographed from the space shuttle* Discovery *in February 1995.*

Gravity

◀ *The Apollo astronauts' steps upon the Moon were the first human experience of another space object's gravity.*

- **Gravity** is the attraction, or pulling force, between all matter.

- **Gravity** is what holds everything on Earth on the ground and stops it flying into space. It holds the Earth together, keeps the Moon orbiting the Earth, and the Earth orbiting the Sun.

- **The force of gravity** is the same everywhere.

- **The force of gravity** depends on mass (the amount of matter in an object) and distance.

- **The more mass an object has**, and the closer it is to another object, the more strongly its gravity pulls.

- **To figure out** the force of gravity between two objects, simply multiply their masses, divide by the distance between them, and then divide by the distance again.

- **Black holes** have the strongest gravitational pull in the entire Universe.

- **The basic laws of gravity** can be used for anything from detecting an invisible planet by studying the flickers in another star's light, to figuring out the flight of a space probe.

- **Einstein's theory of general relativity** shows that gravity not only pulls on matter, but also bends space and even time itself (see Einstein).

- **Orbits are the result** of a perfect balance between the force of gravity on an object (which pulls it inward toward whatever it is orbiting), and its forward momentum (which keeps it flying straight onward).

Light-years

- **Distances in space** are so vast that the fastest thing in the Universe—light—is used to measure them.

- **Speed of light** is about 186,410mi (300,000km) per sec.

- **A light-second** is the distance light travels in a second—981 million ft (299 million m).

- **A light-year** is the distance light travels in one year— 5.9 trillion mi (9.5 trillion km). Light-years are one of the standard distance measurements in astronomy.

- **It takes about eight minutes** for light from the Sun to reach us on Earth.

- **Light takes 5.46 years** to reach us from the Sun's nearest star, Proxima Centauri. The star is 5.46 light-years away—more than 32 trillion mi (51 trillion km).

- **We see Proxima Centauri** as it was 5.46 years ago, because its light takes 5.46 years to reach us.

- **The star Deneb** is 1,800 light-years away, which means we see it as it was when Septimus Severius was ruling in Rome (AD200).

▲ *Distances in space are so vast that they are measured in light-years, the distance light travels in a year.*

- **With powerful telescopes**, astronomers can see galaxies two billion light-years away. This means we see them as they were when the only life forms on Earth were bacteria.

- **Parsecs** may also be used to measure distances. They originally came from parallax shift measurements (see Distances). A light-year is 0.3066 parsecs.

Rotation

▶ *Rotating galaxies are just part of the spinning, moving Universe.*

- **Rotation is the normal motion** (movement) of most space objects. Rotate means "spin."

- **Stars spin**, planets spin, moons spin, and galaxies spin— even atoms spin.

- **Moons rotate** around planets, and planets rotate around stars.

- **The Earth rotates** once every 23.93 hours. This is called its rotation period.

- **We do not feel the Earth's rotation**—that it is hurtling around the Sun, while the Sun whizzes around the galaxy—because we are moving with it.

- **Things rotate because** they have kinetic (movement) energy. They cannot fly away because they are held by gravity, and the only place they can go is around.

- **The fastest rotating planet** is Saturn, which turns right around once every 10.23 hours.

- **The slowest rotating planet** is Venus, which takes 243.01 days to turn around.

- **The Sun takes 25.4 days** to rotate, but since the Earth is going around it too, it seems to take 27.27 days.

> ★ STAR FACT ★
> The fastest spinning objects in the Universe are neutron stars—these can rotate 500 times in just one second!

Uranus

▼ Uranus is the third largest planet in the Solar System—31,760mi (51,118km) across and with a mass 14.54 times that of the Earth's. The planet spins round once every 17.24 hours, but because it is lying almost on its side, this has almost no effect on the length of its day. Instead, this depends on where the planet is in its orbit of the Sun. Like Saturn, Uranus has rings, but they are much thinner and were only detected in 1977. They are made of the darkest material in the Solar System.

- **Uranus is the seventh planet** out from the Sun. Its orbit keeps it 1,108 million mi (1,784 million km) away on average and takes 84 years to complete.

- **Uranus tilts so far on its side** that it seems to roll around the Sun like a gigantic bowling ball. The angle of its tilt is 98°, in fact, so its equator runs top to bottom. This tilt may be the result of a collision with a meteor or another planet a long time ago.

- **In summer on Uranus**, the Sun does not set for 20 years. In winter, darkness lasts for over 20 years. In the fall, the Sun rises and sets every nine hours.

- **Uranus has 15 moons**, all named after characters in William Shakespeare's plays. There are five large moons: Ariel, Umbriel, Titania, Oberon, and Miranda. The ten smaller ones were discovered by the *Voyager 2* space probe in 1986.

- **Uranus's moon Miranda** is the weirdest moon of all. It seems to have been blasted apart, then put itself back together again!

- **Because Uranus is so far from the Sun**, it is very, very cold, with surface temperatures dropping to −346°F (−210°C). Sunlight takes just eight minutes to reach Earth, but 2.5 hours to reach Uranus.

- **Uranus's icy atmosphere** is made of hydrogen and helium. Winds whistle around the planet at over 1,245mph (2,000km/h)— ten times as fast as hurricanes on Earth.

- **Uranus's surface** is an ice-cold ocean of liquid methane (natural gas), thousands of miles deep, which gives the planet its beautiful color. If you fell into this ocean even for a fraction of a second, you would freeze so hard that you would shatter like glass.

- **Uranus is only faintly visible** from Earth. It looks no bigger than a star through a telescope, and was not identified until 1781 (see Herschel).

- **Uranus was named** after Urania, the Ancient Greek goddess of astronomy.

The planet's surface of liquid methane gives it a stunning blue color

Uranus has its own, very faint set of rings

Uranus has an atmosphere of hydrogen and helium gas

★ STAR FACT ★
On Uranus in spring, the Sun sets every nine hours—backward!

Solar eruptions

- **Solar flares** are sudden eruptions on the Sun's surface. They flare up in just a few minutes, then take more than half an hour to die away again.

- **Solar flares reach temperatures** of 18 million °F (10 million °C) and have the energy of a million atom bombs.

- **Solar flares not only send out** heat and radiation, but also streams of charged particles.

- **The solar wind** is the stream of charged particles that shoots out from the Sun in all directions at speeds of over 620,000mph (10 million km/h). It reaches the Earth in 21 hours, but blows far throughout the Solar System.

- **Earth is shielded** from the lethal effects of the solar wind by its magnetic field (see Magnetism).

- **Solar prominences** are gigantic, flame-like tongues of hot hydrogen that sometimes spout out from the Sun.

- **Solar prominences** can reach temperatures of 18,000°F (10,000°C).

- **Every second** the solar wind carries away over a million tons of charged particles from the Sun.

- **Coronal mass ejections** are gigantic eruptions of charged particles from the Sun, creating gusts in the solar wind which set off magnetic storms on Earth.

- **Magnetic storms** are massive hails of charged particles that hit the Earth every few years or so, setting the atmosphere buzzing with electricity.

▼ *Solar prominences can stretch for thousands of miles.*

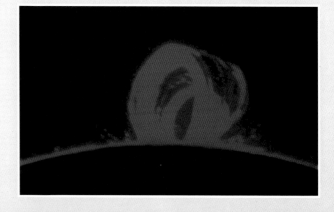

Jupiter's Galilean moons

▲ *Io's yellow glow comes from sulphur, which is spewed as far as 186mi (300km) upward by the moon's volcanoes.*

- **The Galilean moons** are the four biggest of Jupiter's 16 moons. They were discovered by Galileo, centuries before astronomers identified the other, smaller ones.

- **Ganymede is the biggest** of the Galilean moons, 3,273mi (5,268km) across—larger than the planet Mercury.

- **Ganymede looks hard** but under its shell of solid ice is 560mi (900km) of slushy, half-melted ice and water.

- **The second biggest** Galilean moon is Callisto, at 2,986mi (4,806km) across.

- **Callisto is scarred** with craters from bombardments early in the Solar System's life.

- **Io is the third biggest**, at 2,263mi (3,642km) across.

- **Io's surface is a mass of volcanoes**, caused by it being stretched and squeezed by Jupiter's massive gravity.

- **The smallest** of the Galilean moons is Europa, at 1,950mi (3,138km) across.

- **Europa is covered in ice** and looks like a shiny, honey-colored billiard ball from a distance—but a close-up view reveals countless cracks in its surface.

★ **STAR FACT** ★
Space probes will search for life in the deep oceans beneath Europa's icy surface.

Tides

- **Ocean tides** are the twice daily rise and fall of the water level in the Earth's oceans.

- **Ocean tides on Earth are created** by the gravitational pull of the Moon and the Sun.

- **The Moon's pull** creates two bulges in the oceans: one beneath it and one on the opposite side of the Earth.

- **As the Earth spins**, the tidal bulges seem to move around the world, creating two high tides every day.

- **Spring tides** are very high tides that happen when the Sun and Moon are in line, and combine their pull.

- **Neap tides** are small tides that happen when the Sun and Moon are at right angles to the Earth and their pulls are weakened by working against one another.

- **The solid Earth has tides too**, but they are very slight and the Earth moves only about 20in (50cm).

- **Tides are also any upheaval** created by the pull of gravity, as one space object orbits another.

- **Moons orbiting** large planets undergo huge tidal pulls. Jupiter's moon Io is stretched so much that its interior is heated enough to create volcanoes.

- **Whole galaxies** can be affected by tidal pulls, making them stretch this way and that as they are tugged by the gravitational pull of other, passing galaxies.

▼ As the Earth spins beneath the Moon, its oceans and seas are lifted by the Moon's gravity into tides.

Binary stars

◄ In the middle of this picture is the constellation of Cygnus, the Swan, which contains an optical binary star called Albireo—a pair of stars that only appear to be partners, but which are in fact quite some distance apart.

- **Our Sun is alone** in space, but most stars have one, two, or more starry companions.

- **Binaries are double stars**, and there are various kinds.

- **True binary stars** are two stars held together by one another's gravity, which spend their lives whirling around together like a pair of dancers.

- **Optical binaries** are not really binaries at all. They are simply two stars that look as if they are together because they are in roughly the same line of sight from the Earth.

- **Eclipsing binaries** are true binary stars that spin round in exactly the same line of sight from Earth. This means they keep blocking out one another's light.

- **Spectroscopic binaries** are true binaries that spin so closely together that the only way we can tell there are two stars is by changes in color.

- **The star Epsilon** in the constellation of Lyra is called the Double Double, because it is a pair of binaries.

- **Mizar, in the Great Bear,** was the first binary star to be discovered.

- **Mizar's companion Alcor** is an optical binary star.

- **Albireo in Cygnus** is an optical binary visible to the naked eye—one star looks gold, the other, blue.

Halley's comet

▲ *This photograph of Halley's comet was taken in 1986, when it last came close to the Earth.*

- **Halley's comet** is named after the British scientist Edmund Halley (1656–1742).

- **Halley predicted** that this particular comet would return in 1758, 16 years after his death. It was the first time a comet's arrival had been predicted.

- **Halley's comet** orbits the Sun every 76 years.

- **Its orbit** loops between Mercury and Venus, and stretches out beyond Neptune.

- **Halley's comet last** came in sight in 1986. Its next visit will be in 2062.

- **The Chinese** described a visit of Halley's comet as long ago as 240BC.

- **When Halley's comet** was seen in AD837, Chinese astronomers wrote that its head was as bright as Venus and its tail stretched right through the sky.

- **Harold, King of England,** saw the comet in 1066. When he was defeated by William the Conqueror a few months later, people took the comet's visit as an evil omen.

- **Halley's comet** was embroidered on the Bayeux tapestry, which shows Harold's defeat by William.

> ★ STAR FACT ★
> Halley's comet was seen in about 8BC, so some say it was the Bible's Star of Bethlehem.

Asteroids

- **Asteroids** are lumps of rock that orbit the Sun. They are sometimes called the minor planets.

- **Most asteroids** are in the Asteroid belt, which lies between Mars and Jupiter.

- **Some distant asteroids** are made of ice and orbit the Sun beyond Neptune.

- **A few asteroids** come near the Earth. These are called Near Earth Objects (NEOs).

- **The first asteroid to be discovered** was Ceres in 1801. It was detected by Giuseppi Piazzi, one of the Celestial Police whose mission was to find a "missing" planet.

- **Ceres** is the biggest asteroid—584mi (940km) across, and 0.0002 percent the size of Earth.

> ★ STAR FACT ★
> Every 50 million years, the Earth is hit by an asteroid measuring over 6mi (10km) across.

▼ *Most asteroids—more than half a million—orbit the Sun in the Asteroid belt, between Mars and Jupiter.*

Jupiter

Asteroid belt

Mars

- **The *Galileo* space probe** took close-up pictures of the asteroids Ida and Gaspra in 1991 and 1993.

- **There are half a million or so** asteroids bigger than 0.6mi (1km) across. More than 200 asteroids are over 60mi (100km) across.

- **The Trojan asteroids** are groups of asteroids that follow the same orbit as Jupiter. Many are named after warriors in the Ancient Greek tales of the Trojan wars.

Solar changes

- **The Sun is about five billion years old.** As a medium-sized star it will probably live for ten billion years.
- **Over the next few billion years** the Sun will brighten and swell until it is twice as bright and 50 percent bigger.
- **In five billion years**, the Sun's hydrogen fuel will

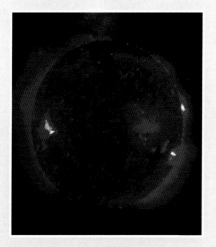

◀ The Sun seems to burn so steadily that we take for granted that it will be equally bright and warm all the time. In the short term, however, its brightness does seem to vary slightly all the time, and over the next five billion years it will probably burn more and more ferociously.

have burned out, and its core will start to shrink.

- **As its core shrinks**, the rest of the Sun will swell up with gases and its surface will become cooler and redder. It will be a red giant star.
- **The Earth will have been burned** to a cinder long before the Sun is big enough to swallow it up completely.
- **The Sun will end** as a white dwarf.
- **The Sun's brightness varies**, but it was unusually dim and had no sunspots between 1645 and 1715—this period is called the Maunder minimum. The Earth suffered the Little Ice Age at this time.
- **More of the chemical carbon-14** is made on Earth when the Sun is more active. The carbon-14 is taken into trees, so scientists can figure out changes in past solar activity by measuring carbon-14 in old wood.
- **The SOHO space observatory** is stationed between the Earth and the Sun, monitoring the Sun to find out about changes in solar activity.

Star birth

▲ Stars are born in vast clouds of dust and gas, like this, the Horsehead nebula.

- **Stars are being born** and dying all over the Universe, and by looking at stars in different stages of their life, astronomers have worked out their life stories.
- **Medium-sized stars** last for about ten billion years. Small stars may last for 200 billion years.

- **Big stars** have short, fierce lives of ten million years.
- **Stars start life** in clouds of gas and dust called nebulae.
- **Inside nebulae**, gravity creates dark clumps called dark nebulae, each clump containing the seeds of a family of stars.
- **As gravity squeezes** the clumps in dark nebulae, they become hot.
- **Smaller clumps** never get very hot and eventually fizzle out. Even if they start burning, they lose surface gas and shrink to wizened, old white dwarf stars.
- **If a larger clump** reaches 18 million °F (10 million °C), hydrogen atoms in its core begin to join together in nuclear reactions, and the baby star starts to glow.
- **In a medium-sized star** like our Sun, the heat of burning hydrogen pushes gas out as fiercely as gravity pulls inward, and the star becomes stable (steady).
- **Medium-sized stars** burn steadily until all of their hydrogen fuel is used up.

Neptune

> ★ STAR FACT ★
> Neptune's moon Triton is the coldest place
> in the Solar System, with surface
> temperatures of −392.8°F (−236°C).

- **Neptune is the eighth** planet out from the Sun, varying in distance from 2,769 to 2,819 million mi (4,456 to 4,537 million km).

- **Neptune was discovered** in 1846 because two mathematicians, John Couch Adams in England and Urbain le Verrier in France, figured out that it must be there because of the effect of its gravity on the movement of Uranus.

- **Neptune is so far** from the Sun that its orbit lasts 164.79 Earth years. Indeed, it has not yet completed one orbit since it was

discovered in 1846.

- **Like Uranus**, Neptune has a surface of icy cold liquid methane (−346°F/−210°C), and an atmosphere of hydrogen and helium.

- **Unlike Uranus**, which is almost perfectly blue, Neptune has white clouds, created by heat inside the planet.

- **Neptune has the strongest winds** in the solar system, blowing at up to 2,300ft (700m) p/sec .

- **Neptune has eight moons**, each named after characters from Ancient Greek myths—Naiad, Thalassa, Despoina, Galatea, Larissa, Proteus, Triton, and Nereid.

- **Neptune's moon Triton** looks like a green melon, while its icecaps of frozen nitrogen look like pink ice cream. It also has volcanoes that erupt fountains of ice.

- **Triton is the only moon** to orbit backward.

▼ Neptune is the fourth largest planet. At 30,775mi (49,528km) across, it is slightly smaller than Uranus, but it is actually a little heavier. Like Uranus, its oceans of incredibly cold liquid methane make it a beautiful shiny blue, although Neptune's surface is a deeper blue than that of Uranus. Again like Uranus, Neptune has a thin layer of rings. But Neptune's are level, and not at right angles to the Sun. Neptune has a Great Dark Spot, like Jupiter's Great Red Spot, where storms whip up swirling clouds.

Great Dark Spot

▶ This photo of Neptune was taken by the Voyager 2 spacecraft in 1989. The Great Dark Spot, and the little white tail of clouds named Scooter by astronomers, are both clearly visible.

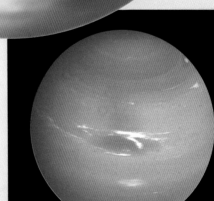

Atoms

- **Atoms are the building blocks** of the Universe, the invisibly small particles from which matter is made.

- **Atoms are so small** that you could fit a billion on the period at the end of this sentence.

- **Atoms** are the very smallest identifiable piece of a chemical element (see Elements).

- **There are** as many different atoms as elements.

- **Atoms are mostly empty space** dotted with tiny sub-atomic particles (subatomic is "smaller than an atom").

- **The core of an atom** is a nucleus made of a cluster of two kinds of subatomic particle: protons and neutrons.

- **Whizzing around the nucleus** are even tinier particles called electrons.

> ★ **STAR FACT** ★
> Quarks came into existence in the very first few seconds of the Universe.

- **Electrons have** a negative electrical charge, and protons have a positive charge, so electrons are held to the nucleus by electrical attraction.

- **Under certain conditions** atoms can be split into over 200 kinds of short-lived subatomic particle. The particles of the nucleus are made from various even tinier particles called quarks.

▶ *This diagram cannot show the buzzing cloud of energy that is a real atom! Electrons (blue) whiz around the nucleus, made of protons (red) and neutrons (green).*

Observatories

- **Observatories** are special places where astronomers study space and, to give the best view of the night sky, most are built on mountaintops far from city lights.

- **One of the largest observatory complexes** is 13,780ft (4,200m) above sea level, in the crater of the extinct Hawaiian volcano, Mauna Kea.

- **In most observatories**, telescopes are housed in a dome-roofed building which turns around so they can keep aiming at the same stars while the Earth rotates.

▶ *The Kitt Peak National Observatory in Arizona.*

- **The oldest existing observatory** is the Tower of the Winds in Athens, Greece, which dates from 100BC.

- **In the imperial observatory** in Beijing, China, there are 500-year-old, bronze astronomical instruments.

- **One of the oldest** working observatories is London's Royal Greenwich Observatory, founded in 1675.

- **The highest observatory** on the Earth is 14,108ft (4,300m) above sea level, at Denver, Colorado.

- **The lowest observatory** is over a mile below sea level, in Homestake Mine, South Dakota. Its "telescope" is actually tanks of cleaning fluid which trap neutrinos from the Sun (see Cosmic rays).

- **The first photographs** of the stars were taken in 1840. Nowadays, most observatories rely on photographs rather than on the eyes of astronomers.

- **Observatory photographs are made** using sensors called Charge-Coupled Devices (CCDs) which give off an electrical signal when struck by light.

Voyagers 1 and 2

▲ Voyager 2 *reached Neptune in 1989, revealing a wealth of new information about this distant planet.*

- **The *Voyagers*** are a pair of unmanned U.S. space probes, launched to explore the outer planets.

- ***Voyager 1*** was launched on September 5, 1977. It flew past Jupiter in March 1979 and Saturn in November 1980, then onward on a curved path that will take it out of the Solar System altogether.

- ***Voyager 2*** travels more slowly. Although launched two weeks earlier than *Voyager 1*, it did not reach Jupiter until July 1979 and Saturn until August 1981.

- **The *Voyagers*** used the "slingshot" of Jupiter's gravity to hurl them onward toward Saturn.

- Voyager 2 **flew past** Uranus in January 1986 and Neptune on August 24, 1989.

- Voyager 2 **took the first** close-up photographs of Uranus and Neptune.

- **The *Voyagers*** revealed volcanoes on Io, one of Jupiter's Galilean moons.

- ***Voyager 2*** found ten unknown moons around Uranus.

- ***Voyager 2*** found six unknown moons and three rings around Neptune.

! NEWS FLASH !
Voyager 2 will beam back data until 2020 as it travels beyond the edges of the Solar System.

Space exploration

- **Space is explored** in two ways: by studying it from Earth using powerful telescopes, and by launching spacecraft to get a closer view.

- **Most space exploration** is by unmanned space probes.

- **The first pictures** of the far side of the Moon were sent back by the *Luna 3* space probe in October 1959.

- **Manned missions** have only reached as far as the Moon, but there may be a manned mission to Mars in 2005.

- **Apollo astronauts** took three days to reach the Moon.

- **No space probe** has ever come back from another planet.

- **Travel to the stars** would take hundreds of years, but one idea is that humans might go there inside gigantic spaceships made from hollowed-out asteroids.

! NEWS FLASH !
NASA may fund research on spacecraft that jump to the stars through wormholes (see Black holes).

- **Another idea is that spacecraft** on long voyages of exploration may be driven along by pulses of laser light.

- **The *Pioneer 10* and *11* probes** carry metal plaques with messages for aliens telling them about us.

▼ *Most space exploration is by unmanned probes, guided by on-board computers and equipped with various devices which feed data back to Earth via radio signals.*

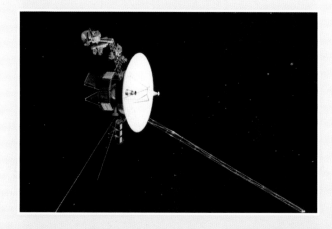

Pluto

- **Pluto was the last** of all the planets to be discovered, and it was only found because it has a slight effect on the orbits of Neptune and Uranus.

- **Pluto is the furthest out** of all the planets, varying from 2,939–4,583 million mi (4,730–7,375 million km) from the Sun.

- **The Sun is so far from Pluto** that if you could stand on the planet's surface, the Sun would look no bigger than a star in Earth's sky and shine no more brightly than the Moon does.

- **Pluto's orbit** is so far from the Sun that it takes 248.54 years just to travel right around once. This means that a year on Pluto lasts almost three Earth centuries. A day, however, lasts just under a week.

- **Pluto has a strange elliptical (oval) orbit** which actually brings it closer to the Sun than Neptune for a year or two every few centuries.

- **Unlike all the other planets** which orbit on exactly the same plane (level) as the Earth, Pluto's orbit cuts across diagonally.

- **While studying** a photo of Pluto in 1978, American astronomer James Christy noticed a bump. This turned out to be a large moon, which was later named Charon.

▼ Pluto is tiny in comparison to the Earth, which is why it was so hard to find. Earth is five times bigger and 500 times as heavy. This illustration shows the relative sizes of the Earth and Pluto.

- **Charon** is about half the size of Pluto and they orbit one another, locked together like a weightlifter's dumbbells. Charon always stays in the same place in Pluto's sky, looking three times as big as our Moon.

- **Unlike the other outer planets**, Pluto is made from rock. But the rock is covered in water, ice, and a thin layer of frozen methane.

Daytime temperatures on Pluto's surface are −364°F (−220°C) or less, so the surface is thought to be coated in frozen methane

▲ This picture of Pluto is entirely imaginary, since it is so small and so far away that even photographs from the Hubble space telescope show no more detail on Pluto's surface than you could see on the surface of a billiard ball. However, a twinkling of starlight around the edge of the planet shows that it must have some kind of atmosphere.

Einstein

▲ Einstein's theory of general relativity was proved right in 1919, when light rays from a distant star just grazing the Sun were measured during an eclipse and shown to be slightly bent.

- **The great scientist Albert Einstein** (1879–1955) is most famous for creating the two theories of relativity.

- **Special relativity** (1905) shows that all measurements are relative, including time and speed. In other words, time and speed depend on where you measure them.

- **The fastest thing in the Universe**, light, is the same speed everywhere and passes at the same speed, no matter where you are or how fast you are going.

- **Special relativity** shows that as things travel faster, they seem to shrink in length and get heavier. Their time stretches too—that is, clocks seem to run slower.

- **The theory of general relativity** (1915) includes the idea of special relativity, but also shows how gravity works.

- **General relativity** shows that gravity's pull is acceleration (speed)—gravity and acceleration are the same.

- **When things are falling** their acceleration cancels out gravity, which is why astronauts in orbit are weightless.

- **If gravity and acceleration** are the same, gravity must bend light rays simply by stretching space (and time).

- **Gravity works by bending space** (and time). "Matter tells space how to bend; space tells matter how to move."

- **General relativity** predicts that light rays from distant stars will be bent by the gravitational pull of stars they pass.

Space telescopes

- **Space telescopes** are launched on satellites so we can study the Universe without interference from Earth's atmosphere.

- **The first space telescope** was Copernicus, sent up in 1972.

- **The most famous** is the Hubble space telescope, launched from a space shuttle in 1990.

- **Different space telescopes** study all the different forms of radiation that make up the electromagnetic spectrum (see Light).

- **The COBE satellite** picks up microwave radiation which may be left over from the Big Bang.

- **The IRAS satellite** studies infrared radiation from objects as small as space dust.

- **Space telescopes** that study ultraviolet rays from the stars include the International Ultraviolet Explorer (IUE), launched in 1978.

- **Helios** is one of many space telescopes studying the Sun.

- **X-rays** can only be picked up by space telescopes such as the Einstein, ROSAT, and RXTE satellites.

- **Gamma rays** can only be picked up by space telescopes like the Compton Gamma-Ray Observatory.

▼ The Hubble space telescope's main mirror was faulty when it was launched, but a replacement was fitted by shuttle astronauts in 1994.

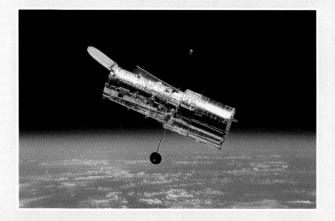

Radio telescopes

- **Radio telescopes** are telescopes that pick up radio waves instead of light waves.

- **Radio telescopes**, like reflecting telescopes (see Telescopes), have a big dish to collect and focus data.

- **At the center of its dish**, a radio telescope has an antenna which picks up radio signals.

- **Because radio waves** are much longer than light waves, radio telescope dishes are very big—often as much as 330ft (100m) across.

- **Instead of one big dish**, some radio telescopes use an array (collection) of small, linked dishes. The further apart the dishes are, the sharper the image.

- **The Very Long Baseline Array** (VLBA) is ten dishes scattered all the way across the United States.

◀ *Many radio telescopes use an array of dishes linked by a process called interferometry.*

- **Radio astronomy** led to the discovery of pulsars and background radiation from the Big Bang.

- **Radio galaxies** are very distant and only faintly visible (if at all), but they can be detected because they give out radio waves.

- **Radio astronomy** proved that the Milky Way is a disk-shaped galaxy with spiraling arms.

★ **STAR FACT** ★
At 1,000ft (305m) across, the Arecibo radio telescope in Puerto Rico is the largest dish telescope in the world.

Astronauts

▼ *To cope with the demands of space missions and to help them deal with weightlessness, astronauts undergo tough physical training. They also spend long hours in simulators and jet aircraft.*

- **The very first astronauts** were jet pilots.

- **Astronauts** must be extremely fit and also have very good eyesight.

- **The American** space agency NASA trains its astronauts at the Johnson Space Center near Houston, Texas.

- **U.S. space shuttles** carry three kinds of astronaut: pilots, mission specialists, and payload specialists.

- **The pilot or commander's job** is to head the mission and control the spacecraft.

- **Mission specialists** are crew members who carry out specific jobs, such as running experiments or going on space walks.

- **Payload specialists** are not NASA astronauts, but scientists and other on-board guests.

- **Astronauts learn** scuba diving to help them deal with space walks.

- **During training**, astronauts experience simulated (imitation) weightlessness—first in a plunging jet aircraft, and then in a water tank. They are also exposed to very high and very low atmospheric pressure.

- **Weightlessness** makes astronauts grow a few inches during a long mission.

Space catalogs

- **Astronomers list the stars** in each constellation according to their brightness, using the Greek alphabet (see constellations). So the brightest star in the constellation of Pegasus is Alpha Pegasi.

- **The first catalog of non-stellar objects** (things other than stars, such as nebulae) was made by astronomer Charles Messier (1730–1817). Objects were named M (for Messier) plus a number. M1 is the Crab nebula.

- **Messier published a list** of 103 objects in 1781, and by 1908 the catalog had grown to 15,000 entries.

- **Many of the objects** originally listed by Messier as nebulae are now known to be galaxies.

- **Today the standard list of non-stellar objects** is the

◄ With such an infinite number of stars, galaxies, and nebulae in the night sky, astronomers need very detailed catalogs so they can locate each object reliably and check whether it has already been investigated.

New General Catalogue of nebulae and star clusters (NGC). First published in 1888, this soon ran to over 13,000 entries.

- **Many objects** are in both the Messier and the NGC and therefore have two numbers.

- **The Andromeda galaxy** is M31 and NGC224.

- **Radio sources** are listed in similar catalogs, such as Cambridge University's 3C catalog.

- **The first quasar** to be discovered was 3C 48.

- **Many pulsars** are now listed according to their position by right ascension and declination (see Celestial sphere).

Space travel

- **The first artificial satellite**, the Soviet *Sputnik 1*, was launched into space in 1957.

- **The first living creature** in space was the dog Laika on-board *Sputnik 2* in 1957. Sadly, she died when the spacecraft's oxygen supply ran out.

- **The first manned space flight** was made in April 1961 by the Soviet cosmonaut Yuri Gagarin, in *Vostok 1*.

- **The first controlled Moon landing** was made by the Soviet *Luna 9*, in February 1966.

- **In 1970, the Soviet *Venera 7*** was the first probe to touch down on another planet.

- **The Soviet robot vehicles**, the Lunokhods, were driven 30mi (47km) across the Moon in the early 1970s.

> **! NEWS FLASH !**
> The Lockheed Martin X33, now a half-sized prototype (model), may make flights into space almost as easy as airplane flights.

- **The coming of the space shuttle** in 1981 made working in orbit much easier.

- **Some cosmonauts** have spent over ten continuous months in space on-board the Mir space station.

- **Cosmonaut Valery Ryumin** traveled 150 million mi (241 million km) in the 362 days he spent onboard Mir.

▶ One problem facing a spacecraft returning to Earth is the heat produced by friction as it re-enters the Earth's atmosphere. Here you can see scorched, heatproof tiles on the underside of the shuttle.

Astronomy

- **Astronomy is the study of the night sky**—from the planets and moons to the stars and galaxies.

- **Astronomy** is the most ancient of all the sciences, dating back tens of thousands of years.

- **The Ancient Egyptians** used their knowledge of astronomy to create their calendar and to align the pyramids.

- **The word astronomy** comes from the Ancient Greek words *astro* meaning "star" and *nomia* meaning "law."

- **Astronomers** use telescopes to study objects far fainter and smaller than can be seen with the naked eye.

- **Space objects** give out other kinds of radiation besides light, and astronomers have special equipment to detect this (see Radio and space telescopes).

- **Professional astronomers** usually study photographs and computer displays instead of staring through telescopes, because most faint space objects only show up on long-exposure photographs.

- **Astronomers can spot** new objects in the night sky by laying a current photograph over an old one and looking for differences.

- **Professional astronomy** involves sophisticated equipment, but amateurs with binoculars can still occasionally make some important discoveries.

▶ Most astronomers work in observatories far from city lights, where they can get a very clear view of the night sky.

Stars

▲ The few thousand stars visible to the naked eye are just a tiny fraction of the trillions in the Universe.

- **Stars are balls** of mainly hydrogen and helium gas.

- **Nuclear reactions** in the heart of stars, like those in atom bombs, generate heat and light.

- **The heart of a star** reaches 60.8 million °F (16 million °C). A grain of sand this hot would kill someone 100mi (150km) away.

- **The gas in stars** is in a special hot state called plasma, which is made of atoms stripped of electrons.

- **In the core of a star**, hydrogen nuclei fuse (join together) to form helium. This nuclear reaction is called a proton-proton chain.

- **Stars twinkle** because we see them through the wafting of the Earth's atmosphere.

- **Astronomers work out how big a star is** from its brightness and its temperature.

- **The size and brightness** of a star depends on its mass (how much gas it is made of). Our Sun is a medium-sized star, and no star has more than 100 times the Sun's mass or less than 6–7 percent of its mass.

- **The coolest stars,** such as Arcturus and Antares, glow reddest. Hotter stars are yellow and white. The hottest are blue-white, like Rigel and Zeta Puppis.

- **The blue supergiant Zeta Puppis** has a surface temperature of 72,000°F (40,000°C), while Rigel's is 18,000°F (10,000°C).

The Sun

- **The Sun** is a medium-sized star measuring 864,948mi (1,392,000km) across—100 times the diameter of the Earth.

- **The Sun weighs** 2,000 trillion trillion tons—about 300,000 times as much as the Earth—even though it is made almost entirely of hydrogen and helium, the lightest gases in the Universe.

- **The Sun's interior** is heated by nuclear reactions to temperatures of 27 million °F (15 million °C).

- **The visible surface layer of the Sun** is called the photosphere. This sea of boiling gas sends out the light and heat we see and feel on Earth.

- **Above the photosphere** is the chromosphere, a thin layer through which dart tongues of flame called spicules, making the chromosphere look like a flaming forest.

- **Above the chromosphere** is the Sun's halo-like corona.

- **The heat from the Sun's interior** erupts on the surface in patches called granules, and gigantic, flame-like tongues of hot gases called solar prominences (see Solar eruptions).

- **The Sun gets hot** because it is so big that the pressure in its core is huge—enough to force the nuclei of hydrogen atoms to fuse (join together), making helium atoms. This nuclear fusion reaction is like a gigantic atom bomb and it releases huge amounts of heat.

- **Halfway out from its center** to its surface, the Su... about as dense as water. Two-thirds of the way ou... as dense as air.

- **The nuclear fusion reactions** in the Sun'... out billions of light photons every minut... Light)— but they take ten million years ... surface.

▶ The Sun is not a simple ball of burning gases. It is made mostly of hydrogen and helium, but has many layers. It has a core, where most heat is made, then a number o... layers building to the flaming chromosp... on its surface. Space observatories like SOH... (Solar and Heliospheric Observatory) have revealed a great deal about the Sun to astronomers.

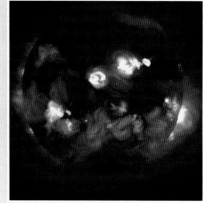

▶ This artificially colored photo was taken by a space satellite and shows the Sun's surface to be a turbulent mass of flames and tongues of hot gases —very different from the even, yellowish ball we see from Earth.

> ★ **STAR FACT** ★
> The temperature of the Sun's surface is 10,832°F (6,000°C). Each inch burns with the brightness of 625,000 candles!

Nuclear energy

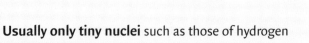

◀ *The extraordinary power locked in the nucleus of atoms is shown when the explosion of an atom bomb releases some of the energy.*

- **Nuclear energy** is the huge amount of energy that holds together the nucleus of every single atom.

- **Nuclear energy** fuels atom bombs and power stations—and every star in the Universe. It can be released either by fisson or fusion.

- **Nuclear fusion** is when nuclear energy is released by the joining together of nuclei—inside stars, where they are squeezed together by gravity, and in hydrogen bombs.

- **Usually only tiny nuclei** such as those of hydrogen and helium fuse (join). Only under extreme pressure in huge, collapsing stars do big nuclei like iron fuse.

- **Nuclear fission** is when nuclear energy is released by the splitting of nuclei. This is the method used in most power stations and in atom bombs.

- **Nuclear fission** involves splitting big nuclei like Uranium-235 and plutonium.

- **When a nucleus splits**, it shoots out gamma rays, neutrons (see Atoms), and intense heat.

- **In an atom bomb** the energy is released in one second.

- **In a power station**, control rods make sure nuclear reactions are slowed and energy released gradually.

> ★ **STAR FACT** ★
> The Hiroshima bomb released 84 trillion joules of energy. A supernova releases 125,000 trillion trillion times as much.

Supernova

- **A supernova** (plural supernovae) is the final, gigantic explosion of a supergiant star at the end of its life.

- **A supernova** lasts for just a week or so, but shines as bright as a galaxy of 100 billion ordinary stars.

- **Supernovae happen** when a supergiant star uses up its hydrogen and helium fuel and shrinks, boosting pressure in its core enough to fuse heavy elements such as iron (see Nuclear energy).

- **When iron begins to fuse** in its core, a star collapses instantly, then rebounds in a mighty explosion.

- **Seen in 1987, supenova 1987A** was the first viewed with the naked eye since Kepler's 1604 sighting.

- **Supernova remnants** (leftovers) are the gigantic, cloudy shells of material swelling out from supernovae.

> ★ **STAR FACT** ★
> Many of the elements that make up your body were forged in supernovae.

- **A supernova** seen by Chinese astronomers in AD184 was thought to be such a bad omen that it sparked off a palace revolution.

- **A dramatic supernova** was seen by Chinese astronomers in AD1054 and left the Crab nebula.

- **Elements heavier** than iron were made in supernovae.

▼ *Seeing a supernova is rare, but at any moment in time there is one happening somewhere in the Universe.*

Red shift

- **When distant galaxies** are moving away from us, the very, very, fast light waves they give off are stretched out behind them, since each bit of the light wave is being sent from a little bit further away.

- **When the light waves** from distant galaxies are stretched out in this way, they look redder. This is called red shift.

- **Red shift** was first described by Czech mathematician Christian Doppler in 1842.

- **Edwin Hubble** showed that a galaxy's red shift is proportional to its distance. So the further away a galaxy is, the greater its red shift, and the faster it must be zooming away from us. This is Hubble's Law.

> ★ STAR FACT ★
> The most distant galaxies (quasars) have red shifts so big that they must be moving away from us at speeds approaching the speed of light!

▶ Massive red shifts reveal that the most distant objects in the Universe are flying away from us at absolutely astonishing speeds—often approaching the speed of light.

- **The increase of red shift** with distance proved that the Universe is growing bigger.

- **Only nearby galaxies** show no red shift at all.

- **The record red shift** is 4.25, from the quasar 8C 1435 + 63. It is 96 percent of the speed of light.

- **Red shift** can be caused by the expansion of the Universe, gravity or the effect of relativity (see Einstein).

- **Black holes** may create large red shifts.

Auroras

- **Auroras** are bright displays of shimmering light that appear at night over the North and South poles.

- **The Aurora Borealis** is the Northern Lights, the aurora that appears above the North Pole.

- **The Aurora Australis** is the Southern Lights, the aurora that appears above the South Pole.

▲ The Northern Lights above the Arctic Circle are among nature's most beautiful sights. Shimmering, dancing curtains of color—bright green rays flashing with red, and streamers of white—blaze into the darkness of the polar night.

- **Auroras are caused** by streams of charged particles from the Sun known as the solar wind (see Solar eruptions) crashing into the gases of the Earth's atmosphere.

- **Oxygen gas glows yellow-green** when it is hit low in the atmosphere, and orange higher up.

- **Nitrogen gas glows** bright red when hit normally, and bright blue when ionized.

- **Auroras form a halo of light** over the poles all the time, but they are usually too faint to see. They flare up brightly when extra bursts of energy reach the Earth's atmosphere from the Sun.

- **Auroras appear at the poles** and nowhere else in the world because there are deep cracks here in the Earth's magnetic field (see Magnetism).

- **Auroras are more spectacular** when the solar wind is blowing strongly.

- **New York and Edinburgh** get an average of ten aurora displays every year.

The Moon

▼ Unlike the Earth's surface, which changes by the hour, the Moon's dusty, crater-pitted surface has remained much the same for billions of years. The only change happens when a meteorite smashes into it and creates a new crater.

▲ The Moon is the only other world that humans have ever set foot on. Because the Moon has no atmosphere or wind, the footprints planted in its dusty surface in 1969 by the Apollo astronauts are still there today, perfectly preserved.

● **Only the side of the Moon** lit by the Sun is bright enough to see. And because we see more of this side each month as the Moon orbits the Earth, and then less again, the Moon seems to change shape. These changes are called the Moon's phases.

● **During the first half of each monthly cycle**, the Moon waxes (grows) from a crescent-shaped new moon to a full moon. During the second half, it wanes (dwindles) back to a crescent-shaped old moon.

● **The Moon** is 238,855mi (384,400km) from the Earth and about 25 percent of Earth's size.

● **The Moon** orbits the Earth once every month, with each orbit taking 27.3 days. It spins around once on its axis every 720 hours.

● **The Moon** is the brightest object in the night sky, but it does not give out any light itself. It shines only because its light-colored surface reflects sunlight.

● **A lunar month** is the time between one full moon and the next. This is slightly longer than the time the Moon takes to orbit the Earth because the Earth is also moving.

● **The Moon has no atmosphere** and its surface is simply gray dust, pitted with craters created by meteorites smashing into it early in its history.

● **On the Moon's surface** are large, dark patches called seas, because that is what people once believed they were. They are, in fact, lava flows from ancient volcanoes.

● **One side of the Moon** is always turned away from us and is called its dark side. This is because the Moon spins around on its axis at exactly the same speed that it orbits the Earth.

> **★ STAR FACT ★**
> The Moon's gravity is 17 percent of the Earth's.
> Astronauts in space suits can jump 13ft (4m) high!

Quasars

- **Quasars** are the most intense sources of light in the Universe. Although no bigger than the Solar System, they glow with the brightness of 100 galaxies.

- **Quasars are the most distant** known objects in the Universe. Even the nearest is billions of light-years away.

- **The most distant quasar** is on the very edges of the known Universe, 12 billion light-years away.

- **Some quasars** are so far away that we see them as they were when the Universe was still in its infancy —20 percent of its current age.

- **Quasar** is short for Quasi-Stellar (star-like) Radio Object. This comes from the fact that the first quasars were detected by the strong radio signals they give out, and also because quasars are so small and bright that at first people thought they looked like stars.

- **Only one of the 200 quasars** now known actually beams out radio signals, so the term Quasi-Stellar Radio Object is in fact misleading!

- **The brightest** quasar is 3C 273, 2 billion light-years away.

- **Quasars** are at the heart of galaxies called "active galaxies."

- **Quasars** may get their energy from a black hole at their core, which draws in matter ferociously.

- **The black hole** in a quasar may pull in matter with the same mass as 100 million Suns.

▲ The Hubble space telescope's clear view of space has given the best-ever photographs of quasars. This is a picture of the quasar PKS2349, billions of light-years away.

Space walks

▲ An astronaut wearing an MMU (Manned Maneuvering Unit) can move completely independently in space.

- **The technical name** for going outside a spacecraft is Extra-Vehicular Activity (EVA).

- **In 1965** Soviet cosmonaut Alexei Leonov was the first person ever to walk in space.

- **The longest spells of EVA** were not by floating in space, but by Apollo astronauts walking on the Moon.

- **The first space walkers** were tied to their spacecraft by life-support cables.

- **Nowadays, most space walkers** use a Manned Maneuvering Unit (MMU)—a huge, rocket-powered backpack that lets them move freely.

- **In 1984**, U.S. astronaut Bruce McCandless was the first person to use an MMU in space.

- **Damages to the *Mir* space station** and other satellites have been repaired by space-walking astronauts.

- **Russian and U.S. astronauts** will perform more than 1,700 hours of space walks when building the International Space Station.

> **! NEWS FLASH !**
> Astronauts on space walks will be aided by a flying robot camera the size of a beach ball.

The night sky

- **The night sky** is brightened by the Moon and twinkling points of light.

- **Most lights** in the sky are stars. But moving, flashing lights may be satellites.

- **The brightest "stars"** in the night sky are not actually stars at all, but the planets Jupiter, Venus, Mars, and Mercury.

- **You can see** about 2,000 stars with the naked eye.

- **The pale band across** the middle of the sky is a side-on view of our own galaxy, the Milky Way.

◄ Look into the night sky and you can see about 2,000 stars twinkling above you (they twinkle because of the shimmering of heat in the Earth's atmosphere). With binoculars, you can see many more. Powerful telescopes reveal not just thousands of stars but millions. Even with the naked eye, though, some of the stars you see are trillions of miles away—and their light takes millions of years to reach us.

- **The pattern of stars** in the sky is fixed, but seems to rotate (turn) through the night sky as the Earth spins.

- **It takes 23 hours 56 minutes** for the star pattern to return to the same place in the sky.

- **As Earth orbits the Sun**, our view of the stars changes and the pattern starts in a different place each night.

- **Different patterns of stars** are seen in the northern hemisphere and the southern hemisphere.

> ★ STAR FACT ★
> You can see another galaxy besides the Milky Way with the naked eye—the Andromeda galaxy, over 214,000 light-years away.

Water

- **Water is the only substance** on Earth which is commonly found as a solid, a liquid, and a gas.

- **Over 70 percent of the Earth's surface** is water-covered.

- **Water is fundamental** (basic) to all life: 70 percent of our bodies is water.

- **Earth is the only planet** in the Solar System to have liquid water on its surface.

- **Neptune has a oceans** of ionized water under its icy surface of helium and hydrogen.

▼ There is a little water on the Moon, but Earth's blue color shows it to be the real water planet of the solar system.

- **Dried-up riverbeds** may show that Mars once had water on its surface. There is sometimes ice at the poles and may be water underground.

- **Jupiter's moon Europa** may have oceans of water beneath its icy surface, and it is a major target in the search for life in the Solar System.

- **In 1998** a space probe found signs of frozen water on the Moon, but they proved false.

- **Water is a compound** of the elements hydrogen and oxygen, with the chemical formula H_2O.

- **Water** is the only substance less dense (heavy) as a solid than as a liquid, which is why ice floats.

Galaxies

- **Galaxies are giant groups** of millions or even trillions of stars. Our own local galaxy is the Milky Way.

- **There may be 20 trillion** galaxies in the Universe.

- **Only three galaxies** are visible to the naked eye from Earth besides the Milky Way: the Large and Small Magellanic clouds, and the Andromeda galaxy.

- **Although galaxies are vast**, they are so far away that they look like fuzzy clouds. Only in 1916 did astronomers realize that they are huge star groups.

- **Spiral galaxies** are spinning, windmill-like galaxies with a dense core and spiraling arms.

- **Barred spiral galaxies** have just two arms. These are linked across the galaxy's middle by a bar from which they trail like water from a spinning garden sprinkler.

> ★ STAR FACT ★
> Galaxies like the Small Magellanic Cloud may be the debris of mighty collisions between galaxies.

- **Elliptical galaxies** are vast, very old, egg-shaped galaxies, made up of as many as a trillion stars.

- **Irregular galaxies** are galaxies with no obvious shape. They may have formed from the debris of galaxies that crashed into each other.

- **Galaxies are often** found in groups called clusters. One cluster may have 30 or so galaxies in it.

▲ Like our own Milky Way and the nearby Andromeda galaxy, many galaxies are spiral in shape, with a dense core of stars and long, whirling arms made up of millions of stars.

Radiation

- **Radiation** is energy shot out at high speed by atoms. There are two main forms: radioactivity and electromagnetic radiation.

- **Radiation either travels as waves** or as tiny particles called photons (see Light).

- **Radioactivity** is when an atom decays (breaks down) and sends out deadly energy such as gamma rays.

- **Nuclear radiation** is the radiation from the radioactivity generated by atom bombs and power stations. In large doses, this can cause radiation sickness and death.

- **Electromagnetic radiation** is electric and magnetic fields (see Magnetism) that move together in tiny bursts of waves or photons.

- **There are different kinds** of electromagnetic radiation, each one with a different wavelength.

- **Gamma rays** are a very short-wave, energetic, and dangerous form of electromagnetic radiation.

- **Radio waves** are a long-wave, low-energy radiation.

- **In between these come** X-rays, ultraviolet rays, visible light, infrared rays, and microwaves.

- **Together these forms of electromagnetic radiation** are called the electromagnetic spectrum. Visible light is the only part of the spectrum we can see with our eyes.

- **All electromagnetic rays** move at the speed of light—186,000mi (300,000km) p/sec.

- **Everything we detect in space** is picked up by the radiation it gives out (see Astronomy, the Big Bang, and Radio telescopes).

◄ The Sun throws out huge quantities of radiation of all kinds. Fortunately, our atmosphere protects us from the worst.

Mars landings

- **In the 1960s and 1970s** the US *Vikings* 1 and 2 and the Soviet *Mars* 3 and 5 probes all reached the surface of Mars.

- *Mars 3* was the first probe to make a soft landing on Mars, on December 2, 1971, and sent back data for 20 seconds before being destroyed by a huge dust storm.

- *Viking 1* sent back the first color pictures from Mars, on July 26, 1976.

- **The aim of the *Viking* missions** was to find signs of life, but there were none. Even so, the *Viking* landers sent back plenty of information about the geology and atmosphere of Mars.

- **On July 4, 1997**, the U.S. *Mars Pathfinder* probe arrived on Mars and at once began beaming back "live" TV pictures from the planet's surface.

- *Mars Pathfinder* used air bags to cushion its landing on the planet's surface.

- **Two days after** the *Pathfinder* landed, it sent out a wheeled robot vehicle called the *Sojourner* to survey the surrounding area.

- **The *Sojourner*** showed a rock-strewn plain which looks as if it were once swept by floods.

- *Pathfinder* and *Sojourner* operated for 83 days and took more than 16,000 photos.

- **Missions to Mars** early in the 21st century will include the first return flight in 2006.

▶ The Mars Pathfinder mission provided many stunning images of the surface of the "red planet," many taken by the Sojourner as it motored over the surface.

Telescopes

▶ This is the kind of reflecting telescope that many amateur astronomers use.

- **Optical telescopes** magnify distant objects by using lenses or mirrors to refract (bend) light rays so they focus (come together).

- **Other telescopes** detect radio waves (see Radio telescopes), X-rays (see X-ray astronomy), or other kinds of electromagnetic radiation (see Radiation).

- **Refracting telescopes** are optical telescopes that use lenses to refract the light rays.

- **Reflecting telescopes** are optical telescopes that refract light rays by reflecting them off curved mirrors.

- **Because the light rays** are folded, reflecting telescopes are shorter and fatter than refracting ones.

- **Most professional astronomers** do not gaze at the stars directly, but pick up what the telescope shows with light sensors called CCDs (see Observatories).

- **Most early discoveries** in astronomy were made with refracting telescopes.

- **Modern observatories** use gigantic reflector dishes made up of hexagons of glass or coated metal.

- **Large telescope dishes** are continually monitored and tweaked by computers to make sure that the reflector's mirrored surface stays completely smooth.

> ★ STAR FACT ★
> Telescope dishes have to be made accurate to within one billionth of an inch.

Star charts

- **Plotting the positions** of the stars in the sky is a phenomenally complex business because there are a vast number of them and because they are at hugely different distances.

- **The first modern star charts** were the German Bonner Durchmusterung (BD) charts of 1859, which show the positions of 324,189 stars. The German word *durchmusterung* means "scanning through."

- **The AGK1 chart** of the German Astronomical was completed in 1912 and showed 454,000 stars.

- **The AGK charts** are now on version AGK3 and remain the standard star chart. They are compiled from photographs.

- **The measurements** of accurate places for huge numbers of stars depends on the careful determination of 1,535 stars in the Fundamental Catalog (FK3).

- **Photometric catalogs** map the stars by magnitude (see star brightness) and color, as well as their position.

- **Photographic star atlases** do not actually plot the position of every star on paper, but include photos of them in place instead.

- **Three main atlases** are popular with astronomers: *Norton's Star Atlas*, which plots all stars visible to the naked eye; the *Tirion Sky Atlas*; and the photographic *Photographischer Stern-Atlas*.

- **Celestial coordinates** are the figures that plot a star's position on a ball-shaped graph (see Celestial sphere). The altazimuth system of coordinates gives a star's position by its altitude (its angle in degrees from the horizon) and its azimuth (its angle in degrees clockwise around the horizon, starting from north). The ecliptic system does the same, using the ecliptic rather than the horizon as a starting point. The equatorial system depends on the celestial equator, and gives figures called right ascensions and declination, just like latitude and longitude on Earth.

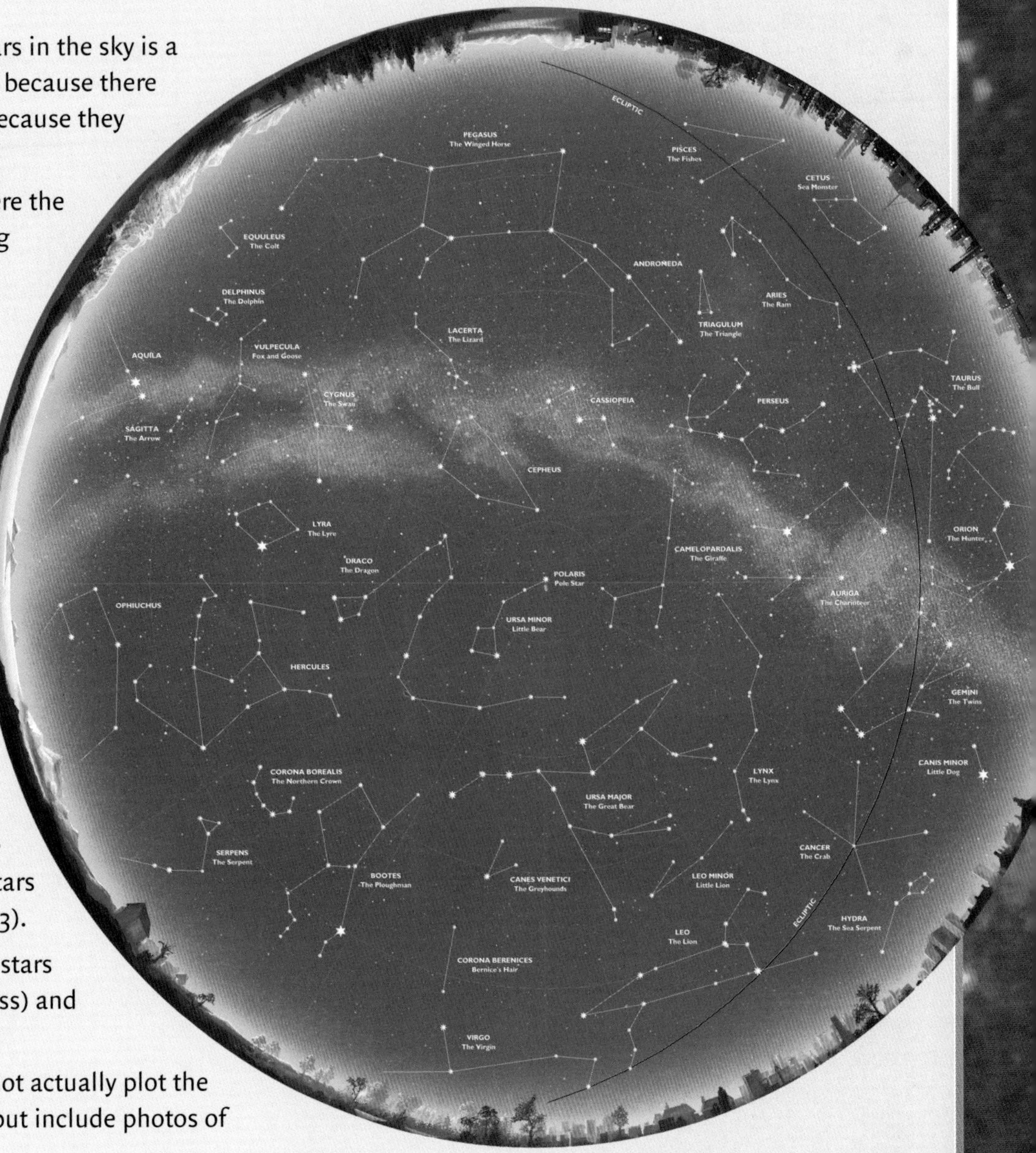

▲ The basic map of the sky shows the 88 constellations that are visible at some time during the year from each hemisphere (half) of the world. This picture shows the northern constellations visible in December.

★ **STAR FACT** ★
The star patterns we call constellations were the basis of the first star charts, dating back to the 2nd millennium BC. Even today astronomers divide the sky into 88 constellations, whose patterns are internationally recognized—even though the names of many constellations are the mythical ones given to them by the astronomers of Ancient Greece.

Planets

▲ Most of the nine planets in our Solar System have been known since ancient times, but in the last few years planets have been found orbiting other, faraway stars.

- **Planets** are globe-shaped space objects that orbit a star such as the Sun.

- **Planets begin life** at the same time as their star, from the leftover clouds of gas and dust.

- **Planets are less than** 20 percent of the size of their star. If they were bigger, they would have become stars.

- **Some planets,** called terrestrial planets, have a surface of solid rock. Others, called gas planets, have a surface of liquid or airy gas.

- **The solar system** has nine planets including Pluto. But Pluto may be an escaped moon or an asteroid, not a planet.

- **Giant planets** have now been detected orbiting stars other than the Sun. These are called extra-solar planets.

- **Extra-solar planets** are too far away to see, but can be detected because they make their star wobble.

- **Most known extra-solar planets** are giants bigger than Jupiter and orbit rapidly as close to their stars as Mercury to the Sun.

- **Improved detection techniques** may reveal smaller planets orbiting further out that might support life.

- **The Kepler space telescope** will scan 100,000 stars for signs of Earth-sized life planets.

Clusters

▲ Space looks like a formless collection of stars and clouds, but all matter tends to cluster together.

- **The Milky Way** belongs to a cluster of 30 galaxies called the Local Group.

- **The Local Group** is 7 million light years across.

- **There are 3 giant spiral galaxies** in the Local Group, plus 15 ellipticals and 13 irregulars, such as the Large Magellanic Cloud.

★ STAR FACT ★
One film of superclusters makes up a vast structure called the Great Wall. It is the largest structure in the Universe—over 700 million light-years long, but just 30 million thick.

- **Beyond the Local Group** are many millions of similar star clusters.

- **The Virgo cluster** is 50 million light-years away and is made up of over 1,000 galaxies.

- **The Local Group plus millions** of other clusters make up a huge group called the Local Supercluster.

- **Other superclusters** are Hercules and Pegasus.

- **Superclusters** are separated by huge voids (empty space), which the superclusters surround like the film around a soap bubble.

- **The voids between superclusters** measure 350 to 400 million light-years across.

Variable stars

- **Variable stars** are stars that do not burn steadily like our Sun, but which flare up and down.

- **Pulsating variables** are stars that pulse almost as if they were breathing. They include the kinds of star known as Cepheid variables and RR Lyrae variables.

- **Cepheid variables** are big, bright stars that pulse with energy, flaring up regularly every 1 to 50 days.

▼ *The constellation of Cygnus, containing a vanishing star.*

- **Cepheid variables** are so predictable in brightness that they make good distance markers (see Distances).

- **RR Lyrae variables** are yellow, supergiant stars near the end of their life, which flicker as their fuel runs down.

- **Mira-type variables** are similar to Mira in Cetus, the Whale, and vary regularly over months or years.

- **RV Tauri variables** are very unpredictable, flaring up and down over changing periods of time.

- **Eclipsing variables** are really eclipsing binaries (see Binary stars). They seem to flare up and down, but in fact are simply one star getting in the way of the other.

- **The Demon Star** is Algol in Perseus. It seems to burn fiercely for 59 hours, become dim, then flare up again ten hours later. It is really an eclipsing binary.

- **The vanishing star** is Chi in Cygnus, the Swan. It can be seen with the naked eye for a few months each year, but then becomes so dim that it cannot be seen, even with a powerful telescope.

Take off

- **The biggest problem** when launching a spacecraft is overcoming the pull of Earth's gravity.

- **To escape Earth's gravity,** a spacecraft must be launched at a particular velocity (speed and direction).

- **The mininum velocity** needed for a spacecraft to combat gravity and stay in orbit around the Earth is called the orbital velocity.

- **When a spacecraft** reaches 140 percent of the orbital velocity, it is going fast enough to break free of Earth's gravity. This is called the escape velocity.

- **The thrust (push)** that launches a spacecraft comes from powerful rockets called launch vehicles.

- **Launch vehicles** are divided into sections called stages, which fall away as their task is done.

- **The first stage** lifts everything off the ground, so its thrust must be greater than the weight of launch vehicle plus spacecraft. It falls away a few minutes after take off.

- **A second stage** is then needed to accelerate the spacecraft toward escape velocity.

- **After the two launch stages** fall away, the spacecraft's own, less powerful rocket motors start.

▶ *A spacecraft cannot use wings to lift it off the ground, as wings only work in the lower atmosphere. Instead, launch rockets must develop a big enough thrust to power them straight upward, overcoming gravity with a mighty blast of heat.*

> ★ STAR FACT ★
> To stay in orbit 125mi (200km) up, a spacecraft has to fly at over 5mi/sec (8km/sec).

Saturn's rings

▲ Saturn's rings are one of the wonders of the solar system, and many people think they make it the most beautiful planet.

- **Saturn's rings** are sets of thin rings of ice, dust, and tiny rocks, which orbit the planet around its equator.

- **The rings shimmer** as their ice is caught by sunlight.

- **The rings** may be fragments of a moon that was torn apart by Saturn's gravity before it formed properly.

> ★ STAR FACT ★
> Saturn's rings are over 168,000mi (270,000km) across, but are only 330ft (100m) thick.

- **Galileo was first** to see Saturn's rings, in 1610. But it was Dutch scientist Christian Huygens (1629–95) who first realized they were rings, in 1659.

- **There are two** main sets of rings: the A and the B rings.

- **The A and B rings** are separated by a gap called the Cassini division after Italian astronomer Jean Cassini (1625–1712), who spotted it in 1675.

- **A third large ring** called the C or *crepe* ring was spotted closer to the planet in 1850.

- **In the 1980s**, space probes revealed many other rings and 10,000 or more ringlets, some just 30ft (10m) wide.

- **The rings are** (in order out from the planet) D, C, B, Cassini division, A, F, G, and E. The A ring has its own gap called the Encke division.

Neutron stars

- **Neutron stars** are incredibly small, superdense stars made mainly of neutrons (see Atoms), with a solid crust made of iron and similar elements.

- **Neutron stars** are just 12mi (20km) across on average, yet weigh as much as the Sun.

- **A tablespoon** of neutron star would weigh about ten billion tons.

- **Neutron stars** form from the central core of a star that has died in a supernova explosion.

- **A star must be more than** 1.4 times as big as a medium-sized star like our Sun to

▶ Neutron stars are tiny, superdense stars that form in supernova explosions, as a star's core collapses within seconds under the huge force of its own immense gravity.

produce a neutron star. This is the Chandrasekhar limit.

- **A star more than three times** as big as the Sun would collapse beyond a neutron star to form a black hole. This is called the Oppenheimer–Volkoff limit.

- **The first evidence** of neutron stars came when pulsars were discovered in the 1960s.

- **Some stars giving out X-rays**, such as Hercules X-1, may be neutron stars. The X-rays come from material from nearby stars squeezed on to their surfaces by their huge gravity.

- **Neutron stars** have very powerful magnetic fields (see Magnetism), over 2,000 times stronger than Earth's, which stretch the atoms out into frizzy "whiskers" on the star's surface.

Years

▶ Our years come from the time the Earth takes to go once round the Sun, so that the Sun appears at the same height in the sky again. But this journey actually takes not an exact number of days but 365 and a fraction. So the calendar gives a year as 365 days, and compensates with leap years and century years.

- **A calendar year is roughly the time** the Earth takes to travel once around the Sun—365 days.

- **The Earth** actually takes 365.24219 days to orbit the Sun. This is called a solar year.

- **To compensate** for the missing 0.242 days, the western calendar adds an extra day in February every fourth (leap) year, but misses out three leap years every four centuries (century years).

- **Measured by the stars** not the Sun, Earth takes 365.25636 days to go around the Sun, because the Sun also moves a little relative to the stars. This is called the sidereal year.

- **Earth's perihelion** is the day its orbit brings it closest to the Sun, January 3.

- **Earth's aphelion** is the day it is furthest from the Sun, July 4.

- **The planet with the shortest year** is Mercury, which whizzes around the Sun in just 88 days.

- **The planet with the longest year** is Pluto, which takes 249 years to orbit the Sun.

- **The planet with the year** closest to Earth's in length is Venus, whose year lasts 225 days.

- **A year on Earth** is the time the Sun takes to return to the same height in the sky at noon.

Zodiac

◀ ▲ *The zodiac signs are imaginary symbols ancient astronomers linked to star patterns, such as Aries and Taurus.*

★ STAR FACT ★
A thirteenth constellation, *Ophiuchus*, now lies in the zodiac. Astrologers ignore it.

- **The zodiac** is the band of constellations the Sun appears to pass in front of during the year, as the Earth orbits the Sun. It lies along the ecliptic.

- **The ecliptic** is the plane (level) of the Earth's orbit around the Sun. The Moon and all planets but Pluto lie in the same plane.

- **The Ancient Greeks** divided the zodiac into 12 parts, named after the constellation they saw in each part. These are the signs of the zodiac.

- **The 12 constellations of the zodiac** are Aries, Taurus, Gemini, Cancer, Leo, Virgo, Libra, Scorpio, Sagittarius, Capricorn, Aquarius, and Pisces.

- **Astrologers** believe that the movements of planets and stars in the Zodiac have an effect on people's lives, but there is no physical evidence whatsoever.

- **For astrologers** all the constellations of the zodiac are equal in size. The ones used by astronomers are not.

- **The Earth has tilted** slightly since ancient times and the constellations no longer correspond to the zodiac.

- **The orbits** of the moon and all the planets (except Pluto) lie within the zodiac.

- **The dates that the Sun** seems to pass in front of each constellation no longer match the dates astrologers use.

Celestial sphere

- **Looking at the stars**, they seem to move across the night sky as though they were painted on the inside of a slowly turning, giant ball. This is the celestial sphere.

- **The northern tip** of the celestial sphere is called the North Celestial Pole.

- **The southern tip** is the South Celestial Pole.

- **The celestial sphere rotates** on an axis which runs between its two celestial poles.

- **There is an equator** around the middle of the celestial sphere, just like Earth's.

- **Stars are positioned** on the celestial sphere by their declination and their right ascension.

- **Declination** is like latitude. It is measured in degrees and shows a star's position between pole and equator.

- **Right ascension** is like longitude. It is measured in hours, minutes, and seconds, and shows how far a star is from a marker called the First Point of Aries.

- **The Pole Star**, Polaris, lies very near the North Celestial Pole.

- **The zenith** is the point on the sphere directly above your head as you look at the night sky.

▶ *The celestial sphere is like a great blue ball dotted with stars, with the Earth in the middle. It is imaginary, but makes it easy to locate stars and constellations. The zodiac is shown on the inset.*

X-rays

▲ *The Sun was the first X-ray source to be discovered.*

- **X-rays** are electromagnetic rays whose waves are shorter than ultraviolet rays and longer than gamma rays (see Radiation).

- **X-rays in space** may be produced by very hot gases well over 1.8 million °F (1 million °C).

- **X-rays are also made** when electrons interact with a magnetic field in synchrotron radiation (see Cosmic rays).

- **X-rays cannot get through** Earth's atmosphere, so astronomers can only detect them using space telescopes such as ROSAT.

- **X-ray sources** are stars and galaxies that give out X-rays.

- **The first and brightest X-ray source** found (apart from the Sun) was the star Scorpius X-1, in 1962. Now tens of thousands are known, although most are weak.

- **The remnants of supernovae** such as the Crab nebula are strong sources of X-rays.

- **The strongest sources of X-rays** in our galaxy are X-ray binaries like Scorpius X-1 and Cygnus X-1 (see Binary stars). Some are thought to contain black holes.

- **X-ray binaries** pump out 1,000 times as much X-ray radiation as the Sun does.

- **X-ray galaxies** harboring big black holes are powerful X-ray sources outside our galaxy.

Sunspots

- **Sunspots are dark spots** on the Sun's surface, 3,632°F (2,000°C) cooler than the rest of the surface.

- **The dark center** of a sunspot is the umbra, the coolest bit of a sunspot. Around it is the lighter penumbra.

▼ *Infrared photographs reveal the dark sunspots that appear on the surface of the Sun.*

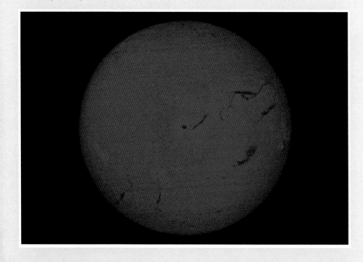

★ STAR FACT ★
The SOHO satellite confirmed that sunspots move faster on the Sun's equator.

- **Sunspots appear in groups** which seem to move across the Sun over two weeks, as the Sun rotates.

- **Individual sunspots** last less than a day.

- **The number of sunspots** reaches a maximum every 11 years. This is called the solar or sunspot cycle.

- **The next sunspot maximum** will be 2012.

- **Earth's weather** may be warmer and stormier when sunspots are at their maximum.

- **Long-term sunspot cycles** are 76 and 180 years, and are almost like the Sun breathing in and out.

- **Observations of the Sun** by satellites such as *Nimbus-7* showed that less heat reaches the Earth from the Sun when sunspots are at a minimum.

The Big Bang

- **The Big Bang explosion** is how scientists think the Universe began some 15 billion years ago.

- **First there was a hot ball** tinier than an atom. This cooled to 1,800 trillion trillion °F or Rankine (1,000 trillion trillion °C or Kelvin) as it grew to football size.

- **A split second later**, a super-force swelled the infant Universe a thousand billion billion billion times. Scientists call this inflation.

- **As it mushroomed out**, the Universe was flooded with energy and matter, and the super-force separated into basic forces such as electricity and gravity.

- **There were no atoms at first**, just tiny particles such as quarks in a dense soup a trillion trillion trillion trillion trillion times denser than water.

- **There was also antimatter**, the mirror image of matter. Antimatter and matter destroy each other when they meet, so they battled it out. Matter just won, but the Universe was left almost empty.

- **After three minutes**, quarks started to fuse (join) to make the smallest atoms, hydrogen. Then hydrogen gas atoms fused to make helium gas atoms.

- **After one million years** the gases began to curdle into strands with dark holes between them.

- **After 300 million years**, the strands clumped into clouds, and then the clouds clumped together to form stars and galaxies.

- **The afterglow of the Big Bang** can still be detected as microwave background radiation coming from all over space (see below).

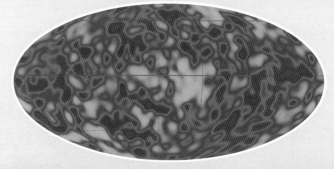

INDEX

Acknowledgments

Artists: Kuo Kang Chen, Rob Jakeway, Mike White

The publishers would like to thank the following sources for the photographs used in this book:

Page 11 (T/R) Genesis photo library; Page 28 (B/L) Genesis photo library; Page 51 (T/R) Genesis photo library; Page 54 (T/R) Genesis photo library; Page 60 (B/R) Corbis.

All other photographs are from MKP Archives